Contents

Page

COHERENCE IN DIVERSITY

Britain's multilingual classroom

Edited by

June Geach with John Broadbent

2396890

371.
97
COH

First published 1989
© 1989 Centre for Information on Language Teaching and Research
ISBN 0 948003 48 0

Cover by Logos Design & Advertising
Printed in Great Britain by Warwick Printing Ltd.

Published by Centre for Information on Language Teaching and Research, Regent's College, Inner Circle, London NW1 4NS

Introduction

This book arises from a seminar *Language and Languages in the Multilingual Secondary School: Co-ordinating Policy and Action* which was held in September 1986 at the University of London Institute of Education, under the joint auspices of CILT and the EC-funded pilot project *Community Languages in the Secondary Curriculum.* The seminar was held to consider the educational response to the linguistic diversity now being met among pupils in multicultural Britain, and to determine practical strategies for acknowledging and using this diversity across the whole curriculum. In a single day only the surface could be scratched; in fact, discussion of the philosophical and educational ethos underlying multilingualism in the schools overshadowed discussion of practical strategies, and no formal report was published. Nevertheless, those who were at the Institute on that Friday represented a growing movement - a movement that is pushing Britain to come to terms with its pluralistic, multicultural society. We were convinced that what we were hearing was not a swan song but a dawn chorus.

In opening the Seminar, John Trim, then Director of CILT, described the educational context in terms of tension between present-day intense mobility of peoples coupled with increased ease of communication through various technical means, and the tendency of the State to impose a unified, standard language on a political community. The issues of the conference put flesh on this analysis.

In 1989 the issues remain largely the same, but the surrounding climate has changed. We have a new Education Reform Act (1988); we have a National Curriculum in which languages feature as a foundation subject; we have the prospect of full entry into the European Community in 1992, with consequent educational, social and economic effects. On a local level, we have a number of government statements and some provision, all of which may afford an opportunity to re-shape our educational world along the lines indicated by the contributions to this book.

The debate on the education of bilingual members of the ethnic minority communities has come to one of its periodic crossroads, and it is timely to have a description of the current education climate, as well as an indication of future development. It is a welcome development that the various sectors of the language field have shown strong signs of wanting to cooperate more fully with each other, and that a number of LEAs have recognised mutuality of interest throughout the language field by appointing advisers designated for bilingualism, or specifically linking modern languages and community languages, and that even where the designation is not explicit, the interest clearly is.

Christopher Brumfit's keynote address, printed in full, is based on four components: the development of mother tongue or dialect; the development of competence in a range of styles of English for educational, work-based, social and public-life purposes; the development of knowledge of the nature of language in a multilingual society; the development of fairly extensive practical competence in at least one language other than one's own.

Section Two is a discussion and response to the keynote address from various sectors of language education. Keith Kirby reflects on principles of curriculum development as they affect all pupils, and goes on to consider specific issues in relation to the bilingual pupil. Exploitation of linguistic diversity as a curriculum resource is seen as an important way forward. The rest of the section is a balance between two English specialists and two foreign language specialists:

Peter Traves traces the history of English teaching which both explains how English (mother tongue) language and literature came to occupy an élite place in the curriculum, and why English teachers are now actively aware of the place of English as a Second Language within the context of language, culture and educational entitlement.

In taking a modern language view, Alan Hornsey provides a blueprint for action, which serves incidentally as an introduction to details in other articles in the section. He urges co-operation across the language spectrum and singles out language awareness as a concept infusing the whole subject curriculum and a basis for further language learning.

Mona Gabb makes the case for extending the role of the ESL teacher in language (and other subject) support; the ESL teacher may be best placed to give this support and to help others to appreciate the nature and needs of the pupils; and both she and Diana Kent (Section Three) consider what connections can be established between community languages and the rest of the curriculum.

Bryden Keenan concludes Section Two with a review of Government statements, and in particular their relationship to language education timetabling, government funding and examinations.

Section Three opens with an article by Laurie Kershook, in which he identifies two main types of bilingual pupil, describes the essential nature of each and the effect on the organisation of the school. This is a general preface to the case studies in the section, which also illustrate the diverse nature of the bilingual or the potentially bilingual pupil according to the nature of the language community to which the pupil belongs.

Lornita Wong notes the widely different teacher perceptions of the same child, depending on the language of interaction, and suggests that this, when added to the social pressures of the home which are in conflict with the values the children encounter in school, may explain the apparent under-achievement of some Chinese pupils.

Bruno Cervi draws a number of practical conclusions about the kind of educational processes which can enhance the pupil's biculturalism and bilingualism; in particular, his survey points to the need for greater recognition of socio-cultural affinities in the teaching of Italian as a community language in order to meet the cultural aspirations both of the community and of pupils maintaining contact with their heritage through the language.

Stella Lewis has carried out a study of the attitudes of pupils and teachers in one London Borough where Urdu has been made an option in the mainstream timetable; the pupils included both those with family connections with Urdu, and those with none, who nevertheless perceived a value in learning it.

Diana Kent reports on various methods of catering for Bengali in the mainstream, and implementing strategies made possible through the placement of Bengali-speaking teachers in schools where a majority of pupils use the language at home, and where account is taken of the needs and purposes of pupils and staff.

Section Four is a survey of desirable policies for implementation in defined areas. Laurie Kershook has put forward the general issues which should not be overlooked when forming a policy, in particular the absolute necessity of involving representatives from all disciplines, academic and administrative, within the school, and provides a checklist against which, for example, teacher trainers and others may measure their efforts.

When this is taken in conjunction with the case studies we may begin to see a blueprint for planners.

John Broadbent's contribution on resources and materials looks at ways of developing the kinds of teaching resources which can allow the policies described by Laurie Kershook to work.

Where John Broadbent deals with material resources, Guy Merchant looks at how to develop human resources through teacher preparation and supply, and makes an overall distinction between the role of bilingual teachers and community language teachers. He discusses the touchstones of good practice in teacher training which are emerging from the EC-funded *Linguistic Diversity in the Primary School Project* of which he was Director. Finally, it is clear that the position of languages other than the main European languages depends heavily on the status they are accorded within recognised qualifications. In his article on assessment of achievement, John Broadbent is principally concerned with how pupils' linguistic skills can formally be recognised in a variety of widely acceptable ways.

It remains only to thank the various authors for their thoughtful and thought-provoking contributions to a vital debate. Particular gratitude is due to John Broadbent who, in addition to making a substantial input to the content of the book gave valuable support throughout the editorial process.

June Geach
September 1989

4

POLICY CONTENT

ERRATUM - *Coherence in Diversity*

We regret the error in the title of the article by Christopher Brumfit on page 7. This should read 'Towards a language policy for multilingual secondary schools'.

owards a policy of
ngual secondary schools

Christopher Brumfit

is paper is to establish a general framework,
t we currently know about the nature of
nature of education, for a language policy in
. Although the title refers to multilingual
, the principles described will apply equally to
hool, though the local circumstances of each
rse result in differences in implementation.
, however, to defend the general position about
opment taken in this paper, so I shall start with
omments before going on to make specific

an only be tentative suggestions. I write from
the Head of a Department of Education,
nitial and in-service teacher education, research
t work. But I do not teach in a multilingual
n to anyone to make suggestions, but the testing
sibility and practicality, the interpretation of
coherence and clarity, can only come from
he proposals to be made here will, even if they
broadly acceptable, have to be developed and
le who are confronted daily with the thousands
jor practical tasks arising out of the multilingual
schools.
need of discussion which is not limited by local
tions. A state educational system, if it is to be
simply be a passive instrument, responding to
aciples or whims of those who happen to be
l pressure groups. Nor can it simply be a free-
nderlying principles. There must be some sense
ondary students being educated in the United
ceiving the same kind of education, with a
imilar sets of values, even if these values conflict
ny in the population. An education that is not
ies purely and selfishly technical, avoiding all
ns of what makes society better or worse, and
ating people as no more than elements in

someone else's grand plan, cogs in someone else's machine. Consequently, the discussion here will ask what sort of principles should underlie the language policy of any secondary school, and will then relate these to the specific needs of schools that are predominantly multilingual.

Similarity and diversity

Language is a universal human faculty which simultaneously joins and divides. Anyone who has watched a small baby will acknowledge our genetic need to communicate and interact with other human beings - right from birth. Anyone who has watched groups of adults going about their normal political and social lives will acknowledge that language is frequently used, intentionally and unintentionally, to confuse and conceal as much as to enlighten and reveal. Insofar as we need to understand and be understood by others in order to be able to operate effectively in the world, or indeed in order to survive at all, language will be public and conventional. It is the tension between these two simultaneous needs that defines many of the difficulties in language work for education. Too much emphasis on the private and personal will create disadvantages in social and public activity. Too much emphasis on the public and social will constrain the development of individuality, and inhibit originality and change, both in communication and ideas.

This tension between similarity and diversity is a necessary feature of any educational system which is committed neither to anarchy nor repression. Whatever our views about the nature of society and schooling in the present political and educational climate, we should, in my view, be defending the need for an educational system midway between these two extremes and what I have to say on language should be seen within this wider educational context.

Language variation and acceptability

Any mid-position will vary at different times in its relationship to the extremes between which it is located. At different times in history, language teaching and language policy in all countries has fluctuated between an emphasis on diversity and an emphasis on unity. Perhaps it is the business of the serious-minded always to ensure that the currently unpopular extreme is defended! Certainly, in language teaching, the case for diversity is far more

Towards a policy of
multilingual secondary schools

Christopher Brumfit

The purpose of this paper is to establish a general framework, informed by what we currently know about the nature of language and the nature of education, for a language policy in secondary schools. Although the title refers to multilingual secondary schools, the principles described will apply equally to any secondary school, though the local circumstances of each school will of course result in differences in implementation.

It is necessary, however, to defend the general position about curriculum development taken in this paper, so I shall start with some general comments before going on to make specific proposals.

First, these can only be tentative suggestions. I write from the position as the Head of a Department of Education, concerned with initial and in-service teacher education, research and development work. But I do not teach in a multilingual school. It is open to anyone to make suggestions, but the testing of these for feasibility and practicality, the interpretation of their relevance, coherence and clarity, can only come from practitioners. The proposals to be made here will, even if they are in principle broadly acceptable, have to be developed and adapted by people who are confronted daily with the thousands of minor and major practical tasks arising out of the multilingual nature of British schools.

Yet there is need of discussion which is not limited by local needs and intentions. A state educational system, if it is to be effective, cannot simply be a passive instrument, responding to the wishes, principles or whims of those who happen to be dominant in local pressure groups. Nor can it simply be a free-for-all without underlying principles. There must be some sense in which all secondary students being educated in the United Kingdom are receiving the same kind of education, with a commitment to similar sets of values, even if these values conflict with those of many in the population. An education that is not normative becomes purely and selfishly technical, avoiding all awkward questions of what makes society better or worse, and consequently treating people as no more than elements in someone else's grand plan, cogs in someone else's machine. Consequently, the discussion here will ask what sort of principles should underlie the language policy of any secondary school, and will then relate these to the specific needs of schools that are predominantly multilingual.

Similarity and diversity

Language is a universal human faculty which simultaneously joins and divides. Anyone who has watched a small baby will acknowledge our genetic need to communicate and interact with other human beings - right from birth. Anyone who has watched groups of adults going about their normal political and social lives will acknowledge that language is frequently used, intentionally and unintentionally, to confuse and conceal as much as to enlighten and reveal. Insofar as we need to understand and be understood by others in order to be able to operate effectively in the world, or indeed in order to survive at all, language will be public and conventional. It is the tension between these two simultaneous needs that defines many of the difficulties in language work for education. Too much emphasis on the private and personal will create disadvantages in social and public activity. Too much emphasis on the public and social will constrain the development of individuality, and inhibit originality and change, both in communication and ideas.

This tension between similarity and diversity is a necessary feature of any educational system which is committed neither to anarchy nor repression. Whatever our views about the nature of society and schooling in the present political and educational climate, we should, in my view, be defending the need for an educational system midway between these two extremes and what I have to say on language should be seen within this wider educational context.

Language variation and acceptability

Any mid-position will vary at different times in its relationship to the extremes between which it is located. At different times in history, language teaching and language policy in all countries has fluctuated between an emphasis on diversity and an emphasis on unity. Perhaps it is the business of the serious-minded always to ensure that the currently unpopular extreme is defended! Certainly, in language teaching, the case for diversity is far more

8

carefully argued than it was even twenty years ago. A wide range of different causes has contributed to our awareness that language varieties are the product of the effective use of any dialect, rather than some sort of awkward anomaly that ought to disappear as soon as possible. Similarly, most countries of the world are now more sensitive to, and in many cases more tolerant of, their major linguistic minorities than they were a few decades ago. In this country, such sensitivity is reflected in discussion of language teaching from most sectors.

The experience of language variety in inner city schools has led many bodies to develop materials for teaching English with more regard for linguistic and related cultural diversity. The work of the Centre for Urban Educational Studies, of the Department of English and Media Studies at the Institute of Education, both in London, and of the National Association for Multicultural Education (NAME) nationally, are examples of this. The underlying ideology of the Bullock Report (1975) led naturally to some aspects of the Swann Report's (1985) willingness to accept linguistic diversity in principle, even if the recommendations lacked practical force. Bullock's emphasis on the value of talk took away the demand for literate (and therefore comparatively inflexible and authoritative) language forms as the pre-eminent basis for school learning. Speech variation is always more conspicuous to the casual observer than that of textbook writing. Bullock's further emphasis on the value of the language brought from home paved the way for a recognition of the value of bilingualism and bidialectalism which is found in later discussion. Acceptance of variation within and across languages is much greater among English teachers than it was even at the time of Bullock in 1975. This may be because of the efforts of linguists and applied linguists such as Stubbs (1976) and Trudgill (1975) as much as of educationalists such as Britton (1970) and Barnes (1976).

Influence of teaching English as a Foreign Language (EFL)

The power of the international market for English as a Foreign Language (EFL) has created a more substantial demand for advanced training and careful consideration of principles - in response to the need for practitioners to be able to work in an enormous range of different sociolinguistic contexts - than in any other sector of language teaching. Much of the theoretical discussion for this market, influenced sometimes by a commitment from the American and European research traditions, has spilt over into other sectors of language teaching. This movement has not been exclusively beneficial, for often the needs of EFL learners, their degree of motivation to learn, and the fact that their teachers have often been native speakers operating at some distance from the culture within which they teach, have resulted in over-rigid structures for teaching programmes, which conflict with other learner needs. Nonetheless, EFL-based discussion has frequently contributed usefully to movements in foreign language teaching of a more traditional kind, and has had some influence on attitudes to bilingual schooling and multilingual classrooms. It has also itself learnt from work in mother-tongue traditions.

A major challenge at the moment is to ensure that insights developed with reference to EFL, deriving from the great input of time and money into investigating its bases and practices, should be analysed and adapted for the needs of other sectors in language teaching. If language learning is a characteristic human activity, the requirements of one type of language teaching must transfer, if interpreted at a high enough level of generality, to the needs of other kinds of language teacher. It would be a sad waste of the past if snobbery or a fear of imperialism led non-EFL branches of language teaching to deride or reject the most substantial body of work on language in education that we have. At the same time, we have to be clear that transfer of ideas cannot be a simple issue, and that the level of generality at which transfer will operate most effectively is fairly high. This is of course a plea for that branch of applied linguistics which is concerned with the nature of language learning and teaching. I believe very strongly that all human beings have similarities that are more significant than their differences, and that the underlying features of language acquisition and language are similar in all cultures. Where there are apparent differences in other cultures these are, in my experience, found to be hidden aspects of our own culture, previously unobserved, but to some extent always there to be discovered. Unless we can talk about language acquisition and language use in a global sense, we shall never be able to help teachers to operate in multilingual and multidialectal classrooms, for language learners everywhere, whatever their circumstances, are engaged on essentially the same task.

None of this is to say that each sector of language teaching should not base its practices on the experiences of effective teachers rather than the recommendations of those in other sectors of language teaching. But the basis for experimentation and development by experienced teachers needs to be the understanding derived from work in other sectors which share their concern for language development within an educational system.

Certainly the impact of work in linguistics and sociolinguistics first affected EFL; it came to ESL in Britain (as distinct from the stronger tradition of ESL in Commonwealth countries), to English teaching and to foreign language teaching in this country rather later. A concern for linguistic variation, for teaching to respond to the differential needs of learners, and for syllabuses to be responsive to the wishes of learners and the meanings they need to express, has been an underlying feature of the 'communicative' movement (Brumfit & Johnson, 1979; Littlewood, 1981). In spite of the necessary and unavoidable range of different (and sometimes contradictory) practices using the cover of this movement within foreign language teaching, EFL and ESL, it is a good example of fruitful influence from a fairly limited number of theoretical discussions. Much of the work in this movement has been a rephrasing, with the sophistication of 1980s linguistics, of preoccupations of language teachers of the past, but it has certainly provided a corrective to an insensitive application of pedagogically crude linguistic models. Furthermore, largely because of this work the teaching of community languages has been able to start from a tradition which provides the basis for linguistic tolerance rather than a rigid view of the nature of language in school and the community. An emphasis on language as use, or on communicative competence, provides a much more satisfactory starting point than an emphasis on language as knowledge. The first forces us to look at links between linguistic repertoires, indeed to the notion of one linguistic repertoire for each learner, with varying degrees of impermeability between different dialects or languages. The latter tends to reinforce the notion that each idealised language is a self-contained and clearly described entity lying somewhere waiting to be studied!

Language awareness

The view of language acquisition and teaching that underlies the argument so far has far-reaching implications for language teaching in schools. In particular, it has implications for our definition of the whole concept of language teaching. It suggests, for example, that learning languages cannot be divorced from an awareness of language as a social and personal system of meaning (Wells, 1981). Even governments are increasingly concerned about the role of language in education (itself perhaps a tribute to lobbies for the values discussed above). To what extent can we separate language learning itself from the general need for language awareness activity in the classroom? Both social and psychological causes lead us to demand increasing language sensitivity from teachers and from society in general. Ultimately, this is a political issue, based on the power structure of society. The effect of a refusal to treat Britain as a multilingual society in educational planning can only be repressive, for it fosters at best dangerous ignorance, and at worst direct exploitation.

Lack of a policy

There is, nonetheless, a problem for educational planning. Schools are not about undirected expansion of whatever is around for learners to latch on to. In language development, as in any other sphere, the school must select from the total cultural store for its curriculum. Only in an anarchic society that repudiated the desire for formal education altogether would a free-for-all be a defensible position. The Swann Report's attitude to community languages is only one of the more recent illustrations of the inevitable selectivity of the school curriculum. What was sad about the attitudes to language in that report was that they emerged in relative ignorance of the complex issues involved, without a clear educational or applied linguistic base from which to make informed judgments at all.

Yet it is perhaps too much to ask that one report should resolve problems that nationally have scarcely been addressed at all. It is not on the whole the British (or at least the England-and-Wales) tradition to have clearly stated educational policies on all curriculum matters.[1] Yet the lack of a clear, even if tacit, policy in language has resulted in the vacuum left by the enormously rapid decline in classics at the more academic end of the curriculum being filled by almost everything except language activity. It does not make any sense for English teaching or

1. The National Curriculum Policy Document has now been published. It could have made a change to the text necessary - but it has not, unfortunately.

foreign language teaching to operate as if the clear definitions of the past have not been challenged by changes in Britain's world role, the different sociolinguistic composition of British society, and the increasingly effective power of democratic movements for minority groups within the great nineteenth century monolithic nations. We need, at the very least, some statements on the kind of linguistic education we should expect for all students. In the rest of this paper I propose to outline an ideal minimum curriculum, within a realistic assessment of the kinds of resources that can be available in the educational system as it currently operates.

Curriculum responses

I shall argue that the linguistic needs and rights of learners could be enshrined in an ideal minimum effective curriculum. This would operate rather like a charter of the state's commitment on language for all pupils (as indeed all state curriculum decisions must operate like a charter). Such a charter would have to include four prime language-based elements for all students:

i) development of mother tongue or dialect;

ii) development of competence in a range of styles of English for educational, work based, social and public-life purposes;

iii) development of knowledge of the nature of language in a multilingual society, including some basic acquaintance with at least two languages from the total range available in education or the community;

iv) development of a fairly extensive practical competence in at least one language other than their own.

In addition, there should be opportunities for those who wish to specialise to work on more than one foreign language. However, I shall not address this issue in this paper, as I am concerned here with the needs of all students, not of any one section of the school population.

I propose to argue that diminution of any of these curriculum elements will inevitably lead to an education which is less

13

democratic than it should be, and that each element will benefit the learner and society in general.

Personal language development

In spite of the fact that the terms 'mother tongue' or 'first language' raise real difficulties, confusing the first language learnt with the language of the home, and with the language in which the speaker feels most at ease, there is still a concept here worth holding on to. All learners who come to school arrive with a language-using capacity which will be used more or less confidently according to how it is valued in school. The situation of each school will be different in the precise nature of language development required, but there are a number of key points which will have to be observed. Pupils (including second language learners) have a right to speak as effectively as they can without frequently being stopped because they commit 'errors', whether these are seen as dialectal divergences from standard English, or interlanguage errors. That is, they have a right to try to formulate their own ideas, in the language they have, without constant interference by teachers in the process of thinking out loud. Only in this way will their own language be extended.

At the same time, insofar as resources permit, learners have a right to language activity in whatever language they find most natural. This activity may involve reading or writing where there is such a demand, either in languages other than English, or in dialects of English. It might even involve local uses of bilingual teaching, if local authorities and head teachers find that to be the best solution. Certainly we must accept that there will be classes where some of the language activity will inevitably be in languages unknown to the teacher, so that relations with local community groups, as well as recruitment of speakers of minority languages into the teaching profession, will contribute to this work.

But the striking implications for multilingual classes should not distract attention from the prime issue. The attitude of teachers to talk particularly, throughout the country, must be tolerant of the language or dialect in which talk comes most naturally, for some of the teaching (Trudgill, 1975). There will never be situations in which teachers will be fluent in all languages relevant to some multilingual classes; there will never be situations in which teachers will be able to speak all the local dialects represented in any class. But teachers can be trained and

14

encouraged to accept and welcome linguistic diversity, and in-service and adviser support can be provided in this process. Already a great deal more happens in this area than a few years ago. But the principles need to spread beyond those largely inner-city-areas where this requirement has been forced on teachers.

There are more resource implications in this proposal than in the others I have to make. But we need to be clear that a child-centred curriculum demands a willingness to address this issue, otherwise we shall only be child-centred for the small minority who use standard English at home. In areas with substantial numbers of speakers of community or heritage languages, the possibility of bilingual programmes similar to that already adopted in the Western Islands of Scotland could be explored (Mitchell et al, 1987).

The aim of this element would not be merely to ensure that a pupil's own language was highly valued. Much more would it be to ensure that the capacities that all students have could be developed to the full. In a sense this requires a two-fold approach: learners should be enabled, without extension, to use their own linguistic resources as flexibly and ambitiously as possible; but secondly, learners should be provided with the opportunity to extend, by exposure to competent users of the same dialect, in speech or in writing, their repertoire of language. For English speakers, this would lead inevitably to our second element.

The advantages of stressing the personal language development element for the learners would be not only increased confidence and competence in their own language, but possibly more effective work in other languages, and certainly a greater personal experience on which to draw in their understanding of language variation and language potential. For society, there would be the basis of a real multicultural development within every community, for language variation is the strongest marker of cultural variation. But far more important to society would be the value of a strong positive identification of schools with the aspirations of parents, local community groups and learners - an aspiration dear to the heart of the present government. There is no evidence to support the view that people learn best by having their base devalued. Confidence in what you come to school with is a far better base for changing, which after all is what we come to school for, than insecurity and suspicion.

A range of styles of English

I doubt whether it is necessary to defend this element at great length, compared with the first one. It should be emphasised, however, that the two are complementary. Any student who leaves school unable to function reasonably effectively in all foreseeable circumstances of social, vocational, and educational need is being disfranchised by the state. Such disfranchisement can only lead, in combination with other factors, to political and social alienation. Nonetheless, it is probably the case that even traditional English classes concentrate over-much on my first element at the expense of this second one. It is in further education that many of these areas are most fully taken up: the fact that they have to be taken up at all there suggests that the views of their job of English teachers are in conflict with the expressed perceptions of many pupils, as well as with colleagues in post-compulsory education.

At the same time, it is by no means clear that traditional ESL teaching has adequately developed the necessary competence in English. Curiously, we could well argue that a combination of the best of the mainstream teaching tradition, concentrating on element one, within the best of the ESL tradition, concentrating on element two, would produce much more what is needed for everyone.

Understanding the nature of language

Understanding of the nature of language in a multilingual society should include basic acquaintance with at least two languages.

There has been a wide-ranging demand for various kinds of understanding of the nature of language. In some strands of teaching, this has resulted in the 'language awareness' movement. Elsewhere, materials such as those produced within the Inner London Education Authority have addressed themselves to the same issue (Raleigh, 1981).

There are a number of reasons for arguing that work in this area should be systematised a little:

a)   Language is to many learners an extremely interesting phenomenon. The material to be studied is all around us, and affects us all.

b)   We all have responsibilities as users of language. As parents, especially, but also as members of any community, we have a responsibility to understand how language is used and can be used. The general lack of understanding of language in our society is well documented: it is one of our major areas of ignorance.

c)   An understanding of what language is like and how it operates assists the learning of foreign languages (and, many would argue, development of one's first language).

This is not the place to propose what should be included in such a syllabus, and work in this area is developing in a number of places. It is worth making a plea, though, for this to be combined with learning the minimal elements of at least two other languages. Now that we have broken with the tradition that language-learning must be an all-or-nothing affair for would-be academic users, we have substantial experience to build on of teaching survival language, or language for clearly defined small-scale purposes. Such teaching, perhaps leading to local certification, may be adapted to the local situation of any school. It would be justified on three grounds: first, as a means of experiencing the process of language learning in unthreatening circumstances, to back up general understanding of language; second, as a way of providing successful language learning strategies, to be developed more fully in a more major commitment to another language in element four; and third, for the practical pay-off of the specific language studied. The languages used might be the languages of minorities in Britain where they are used locally, non-standard dialects where they are well-enough established in the community, conventional school languages like French or German where there is a strong school bias towards those countries, or even Old English or Latin if enthusiastic teachers can persuade learners that there is to be a genuine pay-off. Such teaching could also be oriented towards school trips, and could involve languages such as Norwegian, Flemish, Welsh even where these had justification solely because of local school contacts. In principle, such teaching need depend only on the availability of native speakers, and efficiently trained second language teachers in school, to set up a system - though clearly a great deal of persuading would be necessary in most schools before this could be developed on a large scale.
    Nonetheless, a less ambitious version using materials derived

from schools' existing experience with short-term language courses, would be quite feasible.

Development of practical competence in at least one other language

Quite distinct from what was discussed in the last section, is the need for genuine and extensive experience of another language. This might be French, German, Russian, Spanish or Italian, but there is no reason in principle why it should not be Latin, Greek, Hebrew, Arabic, Chinese or Japanese for some pupils. What is important is that Britain should not be allowed to continue with the complacent assumption that because most of the world uses English as the major language of international communication, language learning is unnecessary for English speakers. Again, this is not the place to explore such arguments at length, and a number of commentaries from CILT have addressed the issue. Let us simply say that the argument about exploitation works in both directions. Many people in the rest of the world learn English to protect themselves against the potential economic and political domination of other English (not necessarily native) speakers; but German, French, Arabic, Russian, and Spanish political interests, to name only a few, have had a major impact on the British economy and political prospects in recent years. How can we possibly look forward to a role in the world where we always address major political issues as unmoving outsiders? The foolishness of such a position should be obvious, and it must be recognised that it puts us out of step with almost all other countries. Because we are already politically marginal is hardly a reason to pride ourselves on wanting to be culturally marginal as well!

Towards a charter of language rights

This, then, is the basis for an ideal minimum curriculum. I have pointed out some of the genuine difficulties that arise in implementing such a programme. Nonetheless, a great deal of the fundamental work has already been done, and continues to be done, by local initiatives in schools throughout the country. We are much nearer the ideal than may seem apparent at first sight, and the difficulties are more administrative than financial. For example, we are unable to make use of the multilingual abilities of many untrained teachers in support of the work done by trained teachers within the system. Only a small number of the moves implied by these suggestions will cost money.

What is extraordinary, though, is the lack of leadership provided by the Department of Education and Science on this general issue. At the same time as we have had Swann, working with only a very limited amount of linguistic expertise or understanding in an area in which (as the report acknowledges) language is the next most important issue to racism, the DES has produced position papers, and Her Majesty's Inspectors have produced curriculum documents, on English and modern languages. For these papers, Swann scarcely exists; indeed curriculum areas other than the traditional English and Foreign Languages scarcely exist. Such references as occur are brief and peripheral. Altogether it is sad that the strengths of these documents are diminished by a narrowness of vision which has led to a great deal of negative comment from many quarters.

Perhaps the DES, like so many of our institutions, is the victim of its own administrative structure. The problem, however, is that it has responsibility for providing such visions of the future as we are ever likely to get. The general lack of vision in all discussions concerned with language is striking, for they appear at best parochial, and at worst as irrelevant to the work that the best teachers are doing.

We cannot afford the degree of fragmentation that such attitudes encourage. As I have tried to argue, it is false to our best informed understanding of the nature of language and language learning, false to the experience of teachers of language, false to the realities of language in British communities, false to the needs of Britain's role in the world. What our learners need is a charter of language learning rights, to prevent them from being disfranchised in Britain and marginalised in the wider world. A possible shape for such a charter is what I have outlined in this paper.

FROM POLICY TO PROVISION

Curriculum development

Keith Kirby

The views expressed in this contribution are personal and do not necessarily reflect those of the School Curriculum Development Committee.[1]

Tempora mutantur et nos mutamur in illis.

Defining curriculum development

Each contribution to this book deals with curriculum development in a general sense, for it is the general business of all who work in education. The question of what should be taught in schools and how it should be organised and delivered is our main professional concern. For classroom teachers it is a daily issue; others may adopt an approach that is more theoretical or detached. Practical curriculum development has often been seen as the working out of theoretical desiderata in classroom terms.

Confusingly, 'curriculum development' also exists as a separate educational specialism and some of us are labelled professional curriculum developers. Work may begin with a diagnosis of what development is required, either broadly or within a specific development to occur and - crucially - spreading the development so that it becomes a part of the system's fabric. Like everyone else - and sometimes more than most - we work inevitably within the framework of national educational policy, for curriculum development in the specialist sense is an activity sponsored by Government.

Charged in 1983 with national responsibility for curriculum development, the School Curriculum Development Committee (SCDC) defined curriculum as *'what children and young people learn (in school) ... and how they are enabled to learn it'.*[2] Curriculum development *'is the organised improvement of the school curriculum for the benefit of children and young people'.*[3] Although SCDC is shortly to be replaced by a National

1. *Ed. Note*: Now the National Curriculum Committee

2. SCDC Annual Report.

3. Ibid.

Curriculum Council, these basic definitions are unlikely to change. They say little, however, about how things will be orchestrated.

Curriculum development and the National Curriculum

Christopher Brumfit has described his curriculum suggestions as 'tentative', commenting:

> *It is open to anyone to make suggestions, but the testing of these for feasibility and practicality, the interpretation of their relevance, coherence and clarity, can only come from practitioners.*

This is an important caveat. Curriculum development does not move efficiently from the centre to the periphery. It is one thing to conceive or devise a better way of doing things, quite another to institutionalise change where it counts - in the nations's classrooms. Where development is centralised, the process of dissemination all too often resembles a game of chinese whispers. The interpretation of the message by its final recipient, the classroom teacher, may bear little relation to what was intended by the sender.

SCDC has achieved significant success by adopting the credo that curriculum development is nothing if not a process in which teachers are involved. In its national projects, expert teams support development by teacher groups on a large scale. Only rarely are the outcomes of this work pupil materials; more often they are descriptions of what occurred, written by teachers for teachers, firmly rooted in the classroom and concerned with pupil-teacher tasks. Dissemination is no longer an encoding and transmission of state-of-the-art methodology, rather a continuous fuelling of development activity. As I have said elsewhere, 'dissemination' should properly be interpreted as scattering seeds around: it does not mean handing out the fruit. This model recognises the relationship between curriculum development and professional development. It recognises that change must be thought through, internalised and owned by teachers if it is to be implemented with success. It recognises teachers' professional status. It recognises too that change is not only challenging but threatening.

The Government has been assiduous in pointing out that a National Curriculum is not a threat to teachers' professional status and this has implications for the future of curriculum development which, in its current state of evolution, is attractive to teachers because of the stimulus it gives to their professional lives. Review and improvement of one's practice prevent stagnation and are rewarding because they offer the practitioner creative involvement, self-determination and self-respect. Central determination of curriculum content is one thing; central determination of the teacher's methodology, the precise means of curriculum delivery, would reduce the teacher's status to that of technician.

Nevertheless, curriculum development in the future will not be quite the same. One reason for this is that development can no longer be open-ended: it must relate directly to attainment targets, assessment and programmes of study. Another reason is the projected time-scale for introduction of the National Curriculum: rapid dissemination of rapid results will be essential. But the most telling reason is a recognition that constraint, changing the rules by which the game is played, is a powerful motivator for development to occur. GCSE has been cited as an example of this principle in action. It is not a close parallel - the readiness of teachers for a desired change is another key factor which must be taken into account - but it establishes the principle. The question remains of how the change process in schools will best be supported.

National projects similar to those established by SCDC may well continue - with certain important adjustments which have yet to be devised - and, given stated policy on modern foreign languages, a 'national languages project' is an obvious early option for the National Curriculum Council (NCC). No longer, however, will they be such an important plank. We may anticipate increased use of the education support grant (ESG) whereby funds are made available on comparatively short timescales to a limited number of local education authorities (LEAs). There is, for example, currently an ESG to support diversification from French. A past weakness in the ESG system has arguably been identifiable at the dissemination stage, a weakness which the NCC is certain to consider: a closer, organic relationship between national projects, ESG activity and the timing of GRIST (Grant-Related In-Service Training) priorities is the obvious and likely conclusion. We may anticipate, too, increased use of the 'cascade' model of training, which allows rapid transmission of new approaches. This will require delicate handling of local support structures to ensure teachers' ability to develop their practice in accordance with each new approach.

Two things are fully clear. Curriculum development must continue to be a process which involves teachers; and curriculum development will occur within the confines of policy.

The Brumfit charter

At the centre of Christopher Brumfit's contribution lies his argument for *'an ideal minimum effective curriculum'* which *'would operate rather like a charter'*. ('Charter' is defined by OED as *'A written document delivered by the sovereign or legislature... granting privileges or recognizing rights'*).

I do not wish to dissent from the ingredients of the charter but would point out that curriculum development must proceed in future under the influence of other imperatives. Those who have read and listened to official statements over the last year will not be unprepared for the notion of a 'minimum effective curriculum' - but they will also recognise that the notion of an 'entitlement' curriculum based on the discrete rights of individual learners, is not the philosophical basis of the Government's initiative. In that sense, though delivered by the legislature with royal assent, the Education Reform Act (1988) is not the charter that Brumfit seeks - and the essential point about the Brumfit charter is that it is unlikely.

It is also the case that much of what Brumfit recommends cannot be addressed because the National Curriculum will be constructed a brick at a time. The charter is framed within a context of linguistic diversity, yet in their policy statement *'Modern Languages in the School Curriculum'* the Secretaries of State have commented: *We intend to consult separately on this issue in due course'* (DES 1985a, para 8).

The limitations imposed by this difficulty on development of the language curriculum are both regrettable and plain. The SCDC response to the consultative 'draft policy statement' commented (para 8):

> *'SCDC welcomes the intention ... to publish a consultative document in the near future on the place community languages should take in the school curriculum. Guidance to schools on this issue will be very helpful and it is to be regretted that this guidance cannot be related, since it is so closely connected, to the guidance on foreign languages in the*

draft policy statement. SCDC hopes that the consultative document will seek to link itself to the present statement. It is also hoped that it will address itself squarely to questions of bilingualism and its implications for learning generally and cognitive development, as well as to its potential contribution to the school's language curriculum.' (para 15)

Despite what may be desirable, the fact remains that the advice given recently by Her Majesty's Inspectors (HMI, 1987) and any developments initiated by the NCC - must perforce view community languages as indistinguishable from foreign languages. If this has a distorting effect, it cannot presently be helped.

This is not to suggest (for it would be ridiculous) that progress cannot be made. Curriculum development is the art of the possible and it is to what is possible that the rest of this chapter is addressed. Each of the four main planks of the Brumfit charter will be explored so as to consider what can in fact be achieved by teachers in the immediate future.

Development of mother tongue or dialect

There can be no doubt that bilingualism is a complex state, that it is a resource rather than a handicap (unless made into one) and that schools have a duty to ensure that children whose first language is not English do in fact become bilingual. Suppressing a first language in an attempt to replace it, through immersion, with English is not a means of encouraging bilingualism and is liable to stunt cognitive development.

In the late 1980s this is not by and large an issue for secondary schools, although it may surface again at some time in the future, as it is presently an issue in the United States. Where it does arise, secondary schools must think through the implications for their own structures of the best primary school practice, for example in reception classes.

Generally, teacher education is needed to inform attitudes to schools languages other than English, and curriculum development may be one of the effective ways of achieving this. At present, many teachers of non-language subjects regard use of languages other than English in the classroom as a threat to discipline, and to their control of lesson pace and direction. The cognitive advantages in terms of the grasping of concepts need to be understood. If they are, the value of acquiring literacy in a

27

first language as well as in English and other similar issues, may also be understood.

Sadly, the entire area is encumbered with prejudices and political stances. Political clout is of more significance than educational desiderata, and principles that are accepted for indigenous British languages somehow fail to extend to those which are seen as exogenous. To understand this it is necessary only to compare the relative treatment of Panjabi and Welsh. Resources are a problem but one that is magnified; the Welsh have shown that such difficulties can be overcome.

The educational needs of community language speakers, and the advantages they offer as a means of enriching the language curriculum of a school, will not be met or capitalised upon until all languages are accorded equivalent status. The public understands instinctively some of the advantages of bilingualism - witness the enthusiasm of many monoglot English parents for bilingual education in Wales - but other attitudes get in the way.

It would, however, be naive to suppose that the present position will change other than very gradually. Where there is a significant group of speakers of a particular language in a school, it is more likely that their needs will receive attention. Where individuals or small groups are isolated, or where a school contains pupils from more than three language communities, the likelihood is much less. These are practical realities.

It is noticeable, however, that where schools have a significant incidence of bilingualism, and where some attempt is made to address this, there can be substantial gains in terms of general awareness and understanding of language - language, that is, *per se* - on the parts of both staff and pupils. Interesting developments have occurred that may be seen to have improved the quality of language education, for example the 'World Languages' course at North Westminster Community School in London. It includes exposure to several languages, low level comparison between them, and serves as a foundation for subsequent language study. Schools which lack the stimulus provided by North Westminster's Babelesque linguistic resources may not have advanced so far in developing their language curricula. The constructive question to ask is how they may be empowered in this respect.

It can only be answered partially in this chapter but, for the reasons cited above, exploitation of linguistic diversity as a curriculum resource is the most positive route forward at this time, building on the policy statement that *'the presence in many localities of significant numbers of people whose mother tongue is not English provides a climate of awareness of languages and opens up interesting and challenging opportunities for language learning'* (DES 1985a, para 8). Further comment will be found in ensuing sections.

A range of styles of English

Clearly this is an important element in a language curriculum, but it is now more than two years since Christopher Brumfit stated that

> *'it is probably the case that even traditional English classes concentrate over-much on my first element at the expense of this second one. It is in further education (FE) that many of these areas are most fully taken up'.*

For its time, my only quarrel with the statement is a strong doubt that what evolved in FE as 'Communications' had advanced very far from the check-listing of a wide range of singularly inauthentic communication acts. However, much development of the school curriculum has since taken place by means of the National Writing Project (NWP,1985-9). Its work may best be summarised by quoting its aim:

> *'It is the aim of the National Writing Project to develop and extend, within the broader field of language skills, the competence of children and young adults to write for a range of purposes and a variety of audiences, in a manner that enhances their growth as individuals, their powers of self-expression, their skill as communicators and their facility as learners'.* (SCDC, 1985).

The search by teachers in 24 authorities for real writing purposes and authentic audiences has already had widespread influence - acknowledged recently in the Kingman report (Kingman, 1988). Attitudes and practice have shifted as a result, not solely as regards the written word, and the Project is now embarking on a conscious 'implementation phase' to advance the process. The Curriculum Working Group in English has given significant attention to evidence from the NWP and - while that Group's first report is not available at the time of writing - the

Project's work is unlikely to be lost in establishing a national curriculum.

In two participating authorities (Inner London Education Authority and Gwynedd) development has focused on bilingual pupils and has explored writing in a range of first languages as well as in English. Thus it may be seen that any large-scale project on language will tend to offer opportunities to develop the language curriculum in its wider sense. Much of what Brumfit considers desirable will also be developed in the National Oracy Project (1987-93) which is open to all authorities (about half are so far involved).

One of the best ways forward for teachers concerned with extending the range of styles of English, or exploring the written and oral needs of bilingual pupils, is to become involved or associated with the work of these two projects, shortly to be inherited by the NCC and likely to influence the national curriculum.

Knowledge of the nature of language in a multilingual society

It is a comfortable reflection that to pursue this element of the charter is to travel with the grain. In his speech to the Eleventh World Congress on Reading, the Secretary of State for Education remarked:

> '*It seems that many children in our schools are ill-equipped ... to understand how language itself works: I refer here to an understanding which is needed for the effective command of the native tongue, and which is also relevant to learning a foreign language.*'

Knowledge about language is listed by HMI in *Curriculum Matters* (HMI 1986, para 57) as one of the four principal aims of English teaching. The Kingman committee was established to inquire into the subject and its report (Kingman, 1988) formed part of the remit of the Curriculum Working Group in English. *Modern Languages in the School Curriculum* stresses the importance of '*links between foreign language teaching and English*', describes '*teaching pupils how to learn a language*' as '*an important element of the school's role*' (MLISC, para 30) and refers to ('*properly conceived*') language awareness as '*an essential part of the foreign language curriculum*' (MLISC, para 58). This last is especially useful in suggesting how to proceed.

Language awareness courses offer the opportunity of drawing together and making coherent the different elements that compose a secondary school's language curriculum. Teaching in the different cubicles of the language curriculum - English, foreign languages, ESL, community languages, classical languages - tends to divergence, which can only confuse pupils and impede development generally. The National Congress on Languages in Education (NCLE) working party on language awareness (Donmall, ed, 1985) comments

> *'Only the pupils who commute in bewilderment from classroom to classroom know what goes on in the different rooms. The language teachers know only what happens in their own room. They consult infrequently, share no agreed vocabulary in which to discuss language.'*

Obviously any curriculum development arising from the Kingman Report (it goes so far as to recommend a National Language Project on the Model of the National Writing Project) must be related closely to other curriculum development in the broad language field. In a section headed 'Co-ordinating language study in schools' Kingman declares:

> *'It can only be sensible for all teachers of language in a school - whether they are teaching French or Latin, English or Panjabi - to ensure that they are using the same framework of description for talking about language and employing the same descriptive vocabulary. It can only be sensible to make overt comparisons between languages which the pupils know, so that they can be led to see the general principles of language structure and use, through a coherent and consistent approach'* (para 4.50).

Yet Kingman's ensuing recommendation that *'all subject departments concerned with the teaching of language in secondary schools ... develop a co-ordinated policy for language teaching'* seems a little too reminiscent of the Bullock call for all secondary school departments to develop a common policy for language across the curriculum. It is well meant but it takes little account of the dynamics of curriculum change.

During the early stages of the National Curriculum, pressures within core and foundation subjects will have a natural 'compartmentalising' effect, excluding each other mutually and also excluding important cross-curriculum concerns like bilingualism. Strategies will be required to offset this and busy teachers are unlikely to evolve successful common policies in the abstract. The natural solution is joint planning and delivery of language awareness courses.

It seems sensible to talk of 'courses' although stated policy dictates they should be invisible, integrated within discrete subjects. Common aims alone would not ensure coherent provision across the language curriculum. Courses might be modular, each subject identifying and offering its own contribution. Joint planning of the overall course would ensure practical identification of common aims while joint delivery - modelled on the best features of team teaching - would foster a common approach and the sharing of techniques.

Kingman observed the potential advantages of language awareness courses ('*In some schools which offer language awareness courses, we have met an enthusiastic openness to language study which we applaud*') but also found that courses '*vary in quality*'. Clearly, insufficient good practice was observed to carry the motion - not that this need cause concern since the investigation was limited and the report can, in any case, only recommend. There is so far but one clear statement of policy, that

> '*provision aimed at developing language awareness should involve the cooperation of at least the English and foreign languages departments and should arise from and be an integral part of their work*' (DES 1985a, para 58).

Curriculum development featuring language awareness has been haphazard and it may be argued that the ideal curriculum has yet to be developed. It is hardly something that is easy to do, and could well be done very badly. Courses must be developed which are motivating in themselves, not dry, where there is a clear relationship with language use. They must be pitched at an appropriate level and planned with care.

Schools have the opportunity to undertake such development within the national curriculum.

One language other than their own

Once again events have overtaken the wish and this objective,

32

happily, needs no promotion. It seems more profitable to turn from it and highlight instead a related point.

Paragraph 30 of *Modern Languages in the School Curriculum* asserts the importance of *'learning how to learn a language'* - which is only partially the same as learning a language *per se.* Transcending the concept of monolithic, single-language study, flexibility is what is required by UK plc. In the working lives of most pupils who will experience the National Curriculum, regardless of academic ability, language learning fitted to precise purposes will occur in measured doses according to need. The infrastructure to meet this demand is already taking shape.

The question is how (beyond developing basic skills and instilling a sense of achievement through study of a single language) schools can provide an adequate foundation to facilitate flexibility. Again, the answer may be found in curriculum development featuring language awareness.

The term 'language awareness' is well defined in the report of the NCLE working party on language awareness, a document that has yet to be acted upon as it deserves. Nine possible objectives of a language awareness course are listed, of which the first three are:

1. *to make explicit and conscious the pupils' intuitive knowledge of their mother tongue;*

2. *to strengthen study skills for the learning of the mother tongue and foreign languages;*

3. *to bring about a perception and understanding of the nature and functions of language with a view to increasing the effectiveness of communication in the mother tongue or in foreign languages.*

The potential of language awareness courses to provide that missing element, a foundation for future language learning, is clear from these descriptions. They capitalise on the implicit knowledge of language structure possessed by all language users and *'can emphasise the linguistic skills already acquired'.*

In developing this foundation role of language awareness, secondary schools should liaise with, and build upon the work of, primary schools (DES 1985a, para 12). Within secondary schools, course development and delivery must be truly cooperative endeavours, not - as so far - led and dominated by the teachers of foreign languages; the emergence as a national issue of what should be known about language, via the report of the Kingman committee, may be timely and serve to boost progress, as indeed may the entire notion of a National Curriculum. Most importantly, linguistic diversity within the school community (pupils, staff and parents) must be used as a resource; not only as the best resource available but because it will foster another kind of language awareness, perhaps better described as languages awareness.

The need is for all teachers concerned with language to participate in a joint process of development and discovery, from which crucible may emerge not a base alloy but alchemical gold. It seems worth the attempt.

The lack of definition of a language curriculum is one of the most intractable problems of the British system. The present re-examination of language teaching offers an opportunity of positive curriculum development, to snatch coherence from the very jaws of diversity.

E pluribus unum.

English, whose English?

The debate about English teaching and the place of second language learners in that debate

Peter Traves

The broad context for the debate

We are at a critical juncture in the history of language teaching. A struggle is taking place about ideas and methods and what is at stake reaches out far beyond the English classroom. At its heart it is a struggle between those who wish to further the aspiration towards greater fulfilment and creative involvement in all aspects of personal and social activity, and those who wish to control and restrain it.

It is not entirely surprising that language should occupy an important position in this struggle. Language is a central concern of human thought and exploration and a principal site of struggle. Knowledge about, and control over language is a powerful force for good or evil. Teachers of language are increasingly aware of this and of the responsibility it places on them.

In Britain, language, and in particular language as the traditional domain of the English teacher, has become the focal point of a highly emotive and explicitly politicised debate about education. Information and misinformation about standards of literacy in particular are the heavy guns in the onslaught on education, educational institutions and educationists. The Kingman Committee of Inquiry (Kingman, 1988) into aspects of English teaching was set up in an atmosphere of crisis about current practice and thought, and was unusual in that its deliberations took place against a background of radical legislation which will include a centrally imposed National Curriculum. English, along with maths and science, will be at the core of that curriculum. Consequently, what happens to English will be of very great importance in our education system. I would argue that its importance goes way beyond that.

English as a Second Language in relation to mainstream English teaching has not occupied much time or space in the argument so far. The place and quality of the education given to second language learners in our English classes is a matter of importance to everyone because it focuses in a particularly sharp manner major issues about the purposes and nature of languages teaching for all pupils. Furthermore, it illustrates the relationship that exists between the kind of language teaching we are prepared to strive for and the kinds of social values and ideals we believe in and ultimately, the kind of social organisation we subscribe to.

A brief historical background of English

We have become accustomed to the fact that English is regarded as having an unquestioned central position in the curriculum. Yet as a subject it is barely a hundred years old. English rose to dominance between approximately 1890 and 1930. In that relatively short period it came from non-existence to a situation where many educationists were claiming not simply that it had a right to a place on the timetable, but that it had a right to the most important place on it. Its privileged position has not been seriously threatened since. What forces produced such a rapid and decisive rise?

I think that we can identify two major forces at work. The first was the general concern for improved levels of literacy in the working populace. English came to claim the major role in the teaching of reading and writing and thus identified itself in the minds of many as a, if not the, major subject in school. To a large extent this identification has continued. Indeed, as the school curriculum has diversified, English has often had to bear an even greater share of responsibility for what is termed 'basic literacy'.

The other force was the teaching of literature, or more accurately of English literature, which around the turn of the century was seen as important in the formation of a national sense of identity. This rather narrow nationalistic justification was later replaced by broader claims for the humanising or civilising qualities encouraged by the reading of 'great' literature.

English as a subject has often had an almost schizophrenic identity. For some teachers in some schools English was identified largely in terms of basic literacy, and this developed into the highly structured teaching of grammar, punctuation and spelling that characterised so much of the English syllabus well into the 1960s. For other teachers, usually in other schools, English lessons were seen as an opportunity for the teaching of literature. These teachers saw literature as having a central role in the maintenance or restoration of civilisation. Leavis' work represents a lucid account of the second view. Interestingly, both the grammatical and the literary work rose to pre-eminence during a period when very little serious linguistic study (with the notable exception of Firth) was taking place in Britain.

By the 1960s a new generation of teachers had come to believe that the reading of good literature encouraged the development of sensibilities which would resist the crude materialism of mass culture. They saw great literature as being 'life enhancing' in the intelligent and critical reader. A little later these were followed by a new generation of teachers, equally committed to the development of personal sensibilities, but who shifted the point of concern from the reception of literature to the child's creative use of language.

For many years these teachers represented a spirited, intelligent and determined opposition to crudely utilitarian approaches to language work. Both models attempted to assert human worth in the face of great pressure for a ruthless concentration on basic skills, on education to meet the needs of the economy. It also needs to be recognised that to a considerable extent the dominant theory and practice of classroom English is still informed by these two traditions of thought.

The multicultural dimension

A number of less general but nevertheless important developments have taken place over the last fifteen years or so. Among these have been an increased concern in some schools to validate and represent the culture of working class children. This has expressed itself both in the literature used and in the encouragement given to children to draw on and value their own experience. Multicultural education represents, in part at least, a broadening out of this tendency in an attempt to recognise and celebrate the culturally plural nature of classrooms and of society itself. Although multicultural education has received a great deal of attention and a considerable amount of lip service, it is likely that good practice is still limited to relatively few schools and authorities. The validation of working class experience has been equally if not more limited in the scale of its achievement.

Two movements wider in reference than just English have had a notable effect on practice and theory within the subject. These are mixed ability teaching and child-centred education, both of which have had a marked effect on the kind of work done in English. It has affected the kind of writing encouraged, the type of literature read and the value ascribed to talk in the classroom.

Increasingly there has been a belief that if children are to improve and increase their facility in a language, their own linguistic and cultural background needs to be acknowledged and valued, a view embodied in the report of the Bullock Committee (Bullock, 1975) which embodied a great deal of this consensus. More recently a growing awareness of linguistic and literacy theories, originating largely in Europe, has produced questioning within English of its liberal-humanist and predominantly individualistic base. Greater attention has begun to be paid to the fact that language is a socially and historically situated phenomenon and that the production of meaning is an immensely complex business. Of far greater immediate importance, however, is the renewed spirit of utilitarianism abroad in the country. The Philistine demands for a 'back to basics' curriculum are combined with a 'little England' ethos that sneers at linguistic and cultural plurality. In the face of such a formidable attack there has been a dramatic loss of confidence and a sense of bewilderment among English teachers. It is in this context that many of them are being faced with English-as-second-language learners in their mainstream classes. Their response will be a crucial test of the depth of their convictions about what has been, and can be achieved in language and literature work.

Second language learners in mainstream English classrooms

The experience of English teachers with regard to second language learners is very varied. It should come as no surprise that the response made by English teachers has been equally varied.

In the past many English teachers were extremely reluctant to take responsibility for students who were beginners in English. It is probable that this approach is still fairly prevalent, though it is arguable that English teachers are less likely to take this line than many of their colleagues in other subject areas. Nevertheless, it has to be admitted that a great deal of the old ignorance and confusion still exists. At the heart of the problem is a mixture of anxiety, fear and guilt. Many English teachers are anxious about their ability to help second language learners. They acknowledge, and in many ways are demoralised by, a body of knowledge and expertise known either as Teaching English as a Foreign Language or Teaching English as a Second Language. There is a strong tendency to look to outside experts to do the job. They are afraid of a situation in which their own expertise is called into question and feel guilty about their own inability to help children in their classes. This is compounded by real ignorance about the linguistic resources of these children. It is still not unknown for English teachers to speak of children who are fluent in, say, Panjabi and Urdu and who can make themselves understood with difficulty in English, as having little or even no language. Nor is it uncommon for schools to confuse the support needed by second language learners with that needed by children with learning difficulties, particularly in the areas of reading and writing. The insidious effect this confusion is likely to have on the perception of those children by both staff and other students does not need to be spelt out here.

Second language learners have been, and to a large extent still are, regarded as a problem. Furthermore, they are not seen as a problem that is likely to be addressed effectively by the areas of knowledge that English teachers consider themselves as being experts in. Indeed, one of the sadder facts is the way in which English teachers forget or lose confidence in what they know about language, language acquisition and literacy when faced with students who do not have English as a first language. A great deal of progress has been made, nevertheless, on the issue of second language learners in mainstream English classes. My only concern is a nagging doubt about how widespread this progress has been. The progress that has been made on such issues as valuing the child's culture and language, the acceptance of the importance of purposeful talk in the classroom, and a more subtle and constructive approach to the encouragement and assessment of writing, ought to provide a firm foundation for English teachers to build on. They need to have the confidence to do so when working with second language learners. There is also a growing awareness that the monolingual or monocultural classroom is itself an illusion. All language users have complex personal family histories of language use and register. This is an area of interest and work that can be and is being developed, and should be of great use to teachers in all kinds of schools.

Problems still exist even where good theory and practice have made inroads. The models of good practice easily available to teachers do not always seem immediately applicable to their own classrooms. Suggestions for materials or methodology based on the assumption of three, four or five second language learners in a class may not appear helpful to the teacher who has classes where the great majority, or even all of the students, are beginners or near beginners in English. Good practice also demands a high level of resourcing both in terms of teachers and materials. These resources are not always forthcoming. The dissemination of good theory and practice has not been as widespread or as effective as it should have been and there is still a tendency for schools or authorities to respond to the issue only when they feel threatened or pressurised by the presence of large numbers of second language learners. The greatest problem of all, however, is the current crisis in education in general, and in language teaching in particular.

The current debate

I would like now to go on and examine the place of English as a Second Language in this debate, setting it within the context of wider issues about language, culture and educational entitlement. In his speech at Pangbourne in 1986 when he announced the setting up of the Kingman Committee, the Secretary of State for Education and Science, Mr Baker, emphasised the capacity of language to unite. In particular, he stressed the importance of English as a means of unifying peoples from disparate backgrounds and far-flung parts of the world within a homogeneous national identity. Language does have the power to unify, to draw together and identify. It is true that a sense of 'Englishness' cannot be separated from the history of English as a language. Language can also, however, divide, set apart and oppress. English has not developed in a uniform and obviously coherent manner. The various dialects have not achieved equal status. Differences in class, gender and race have been perpetuated. This would not be a problem if the differences were constructed in terms of a valued plurality. Such is not the case. The differences are perceived not in terms of kind or type, but rather in terms of their proximity to the dominant norm. Class, race and gender are a part of the hierarchical structure of our society, in which wealth and power are unequally distributed. Language is one of the most effective means by which this ordering is achieved. Consequently, language is a major site of ideological struggle.

The second language learner has a particularly significant place in this struggle. The education system tends to use the second language situation as a justification for the underachievement of large numbers of students. This kind of justification is a gross over-simplification of the issues involved, ignoring as it does other factors such as the hostile attitude often exhibited towards the race and culture of second language learners. It needs to be remembered, furthermore, that many second language learners are concentrated in areas of industrial and economic decay. All children need to see their culture and their language valued if they are to be effective and confident learners. The attitude and approach of teachers, particularly English teachers, to second language learners is an accurate measurement of the extent to which they have taken on the validation of the linguistic and cultural background of all children.

What we need to assert as English teachers is the concept of entitlement. This is an idea stressed by Christopher Brumfit in the opening article. In terms of English teaching this means a commitment to the right of all children to the fullest possible form of critical and creative literacy. Included in this would be a right to competence in, and a working knowledge about, various forms of English. Of particular importance would be the capacity to express oneself clearly and accurately in Standard English and to recognise the need to vary the register of spoken English according to the demands of different situations.[1] The success or failure of second language learners in this endeavour will give us a good indication of more general progress or regress. Such a view of entitlement cannot be rooted in the crudest definitions of economic necessity. It must be seen as part of a broader attempt to enfranchise people, to empower them to play the largest possible role in the control of their own personal lives and in the social, political, economic and cultural life of society. If language is truly to serve the unifying function that Mr Baker believes it has played, then there will be a paradoxically greater need to begin by valuing the cultural and linguistic diversity present in our classroom and our society. But that by itself will not be enough. We must also fight for the resources to ensure that no

1. *Ed note*: Report from Cox, B, Chairman: *English for ages 5 to 11*. London: National Curriculum Council, 1988. See glossary.

child, second language learners included, is denied his or her linguistic entitlement, which forms a vital part of the broader educational entitlement we must aim for.

An ESL perspective for community languages in the curriculum

Mona Gabb

In order to lay the foundation of a genuinely pluralist society, the education system must cater for the linguistic needs of ethnic minority pupils, take full advantage of the opportunities offered and tap the resources of a linguistically diverse society. Do we regard this diversity as a 'problem'? Surely it should be viewed as a rich resource which can only heighten pupils' awareness of linguistic diversity and foster a real understanding of the role and function of language in all its forms, but all too often it falls to the ESL specialist to attempt to convince colleagues of the linguistic advantages of being bilingual.

It is important to acknowledge and respect these bilingual skills and the ESL specialist can help to encourage teachers not only consciously to use the languages, but to help identify the different languages and dialects used by the pupils. In his ideal charter, Christopher Brumfit argues that the linguistic needs of the learner should include development of competence in a range of styles of English, and this should be part of the concern of the ESL specialist in the multi-disciplinary role of support work across the mainstream curriculum. English as a Second Language support suggests a relatively new element for the policy: if a strategy of delivering the curriculum at the same time as developing language can succeed for English, could the strategy not also be applicable to the other languages which pupils already know?

The contribution of the second language teacher

Over the past few years, the role of the ESL specialist in schools has tended to move away from the direct teaching of English in withdrawal situations, to the shouldering of a wider range of responsibilities within the school community, with the central aim of supporting the educational experiences of bilingual children. It is argued that children who are learning to use English in England are best integrated into regular school activities from the start, since for them English is best taught within the context of other school subjects. This practice does not, of course, obviate the need for members of staff in

43

multilingual schools to seek to develop special relationships with pupils who are relatively unfamiliar with English as medium of instruction.

The main emphasis has moved into the maintenance of morale at difficult stages of language acquisition. It has been recognised that the main motivation for learning to speak a language is the need to communicate, and consequently that in the school context the most appropriate and motivating language learning situation may well be with a group of peers in a mainstream classroom: children make excellent teachers and guides.

The role of the ESL teacher becomes extended to acting as a reference point for other teachers with bilingual children in their classes who may need help in order to meet the demands of the curriculum; to discussing strategies which could provide for more effective learning within the classroom; and to identifying the curriculum areas which cause the greatest difficulty, with a view to eliminating the problems through curriculum development. In general it would seem that activities that are good for students learning English as a new language are often good for all our students.

Acknowledging bilingualism

Recent educational research has produced considerable evidence to suggest that bilingualism can benefit children's overall academic and intellectual progress. We know that supporting the development of a child's first language will enhance the learning of a second, and that concepts developed in the first language can be easily transferred to a second. Bilingualism can moreover be a positive force in social and conceptual development, especially where the first languages of pupils are promoted by the school. Unfortunately, since teachers of English as a Second Language are faced with the dilemma that our interaction with pupils is intended so specifically to produce improvements in the pupils' use of English, we often dare not risk using valuable contact time with pupils for underpinning the language and culture of the home. It may be that in schools where the pupils' languages, and we ourselves as teachers, are perceived as being of diminished status in relation to the rest of the curriculum and to the more established teachers, any intervention which we attempt will result in our rejection by the very pupils we are attempting to help.

This negative syndrome need not necessarily be irreversible. By and large we know we are operating effectively when we can provide a nexus between the child as formed by the home background, and successful school learning. It is our sympathetic concern for their progress which can overcome the moments of frustration in their bilingual development in a society made rigid with such monolingual norms. In challenging these norms we are automatically enhancing the learning environment for all pupils and not solely for those who are already bilingual.

The way forward lies in the permutation of an effective partnership between pupil, teacher, parent and the wider community; for example, through a programme of language and culture support within the school, which may well lead to the active recruitment of bilingual teachers and the acquisition of at least basic knowledge of a community language by a monolingual teacher. The role of teacher for English as a Second Language is therefore not for the teacher who is faint of heart or lacking in commitment!

All secondary schools, including apparently monolingual schools, should seek to foster amongst pupils an awareness of language diversity, including the dialect repertoires of the children.

In both multilingual and monolingual schools, a survey of the language competencies within the school could usefully underlie the development of a school language policy, which would then find partial expression in a language awareness programme. (See pages 107ff for L Kershook's discussion of such a programme.)

Supporting bilingualism

How do we encourage the use of home languages in a secondary school even if most of the teaching staff are monolingual? Ideally, bilingual education should encourage the use of pupils' home language as a medium for instruction alongside English, so that the child may be taught for a set part of the day in, for example, Gujarati, and the rest of the time in English. It would be possible to teach a subject in the home language or teach the whole curriculum for parts of the day in the home language. There are a number of interesting precedents of schools in which the national language has been rejected in favour of an alternative medium of instruction. For example, in the Soviet Union and in India, certain schools are English medium schools. In anglophone areas of Canada, subjects can be taught in French.

Other than in Wales, the British educational establishment has not yet systematically addressed the issue of bilingual teachers teaching subjects in two languages.

Acknowledgement of individual cultural and linguistic variation is encouraged by relating the curriculum to the children's own experience. Cross-curricular links through the language support teacher, for example, in home economics, history or geography, will also give the pupils opportunities to draw upon their own experiences. The ESL teacher can thus help to develop a policy to enable practical strategies for language awareness and the encouragement of bilingualism to be implemented and take the lead in arguing for the curriculum to contain the languages of the pupils as part of the secondary school curriculum.

Figures 1, 2 and 3 illustrate respectively, a model structure of a support teacher's work in administrative, cross-curricular, and cross-subject terms. Within this framework, the learners work at developing a competence and range of styles of English for educational needs and social skills for life. Within the subject area a knowledge of the nature of language in a multilingual society is fostered. Diagrams on pp 63a-c.

Community languages and modern languages

The language of the community is a potent symbolic representation of culture: to accept the languages is part way to accepting the cultures. How can we put community languages on the agenda in the modern languages department of the secondary school? Ideally, there should be an opportunity for pupils to select two languages.

There may be certain universals common to all languages; while the actual terms used for certain ideas may vary from language to language, the range of significance of these equivalent terms tends to be very similar, so that to a large extent the vocabulary of one language may well be a psychological and cultural translation of the vocabulary of another.

If community languages are included in the modern languages curriculum along with French and German, the ESL teacher again has a role to show the relevance of ESL procedures, especially the way in which awareness of the learner's competence and situation can be taken into account. This would mean, for example, a divergence from the accepted practice in foreign language teaching of reliance on the use of English in the classroom to teach the languages, and in examinations to put the questions, both practices which penalise the bilingual learner who has an imperfect grasp of English.

It is an important function for the ESL teacher to be a natural channel for discussion and initiatives. The ESL teacher needs to seek and develop institutional structures across language provision in schools to facilitate intervention. Such intervention may take the form as suggested above of methodological cross-fertilisation or, as suggested below, might result in forms of profiling which are consistent across language disciplines.

Compiling records of achievement for bilingual pupils

As records of achievement become an intrinsic part of pupils' needs for career and further education, it is apparent that some pupils will need support to improve their understanding of objectives, targets and progress. It is essential that part of the diagnostic interviews be carried out in the home language: to expand the depth of the interview in this way helps to encourage students to record achievements and identify skills which they possess but may not yet have demonstrated in the classroom. It is important to include on the summative document some evidence of the pupil's cultural background in order to demonstrate the full range of skills, both as recognition for the student and as valuable information for the potential user of the document.

What else can teachers of English as a Second Language do to help students to produce a complete summative document? All teachers should recognise that the value placed on particular personal and social qualities will vary between cultures and according to the individual. Attitudes and values transmitted in some students' upbringing may be in conflict with those promoted by teachers. Muslim families, for example, may not wish to allow girls to stay late for after-school activities, although teachers may insist that such activities are a valuable part of school life. Demonstration of some skills, for example problem-solving or information handling, may be difficult for students with little English.

The records of achievement will accompany pupils throughout their school career. In addition to helping pupils to realise their full potential, motivating them by recording steady

Figure 1

CURRICULUM DEVELOPMENT : WORK STRUCTURE

PLANNING

a) Liaising with postholders and Heads of
Department Re: Content, Context, Educational
Aims and Time-tabling

TEAM TEACHING

a) Classroom teaching, Workshops, Lectures
b) Development of backing materials at
Resources Centre

EVALUATION

Exhibitions, assemblies, performances, meeting parents
and whole staff - Governors Report, Working Party
material.

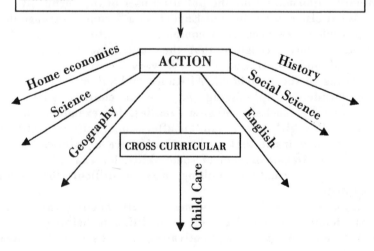

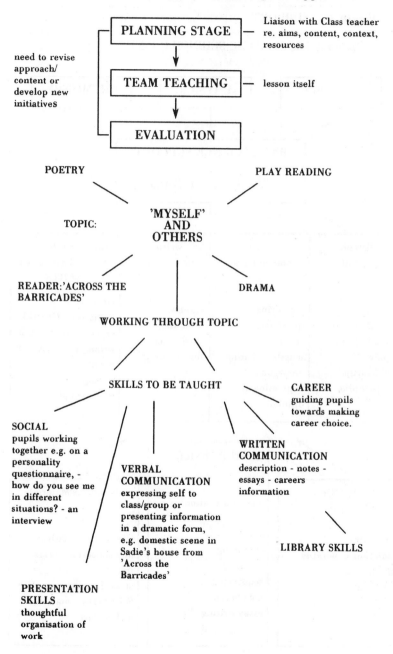

Figure 2 English: C.S.E. English Support

PLANNING STAGE

Liaison with Class teacher re. aims, content, context, resources

TEAM TEACHING

lesson itself

EVALUATION

need to revise approach/content or develop new initiatives

POETRY

PLAY READING

TOPIC:

'MYSELF' AND OTHERS

READER:'ACROSS THE BARRICADES'

DRAMA

WORKING THROUGH TOPIC

SKILLS TO BE TAUGHT

CAREER guiding pupils towards making career choice.

SOCIAL pupils working together e.g. on a personality questionnaire, - how do you see me in different situations? - an interview

VERBAL COMMUNICATION expressing self to class/group or presenting information in a dramatic form, e.g. domestic scene in Sadie's house from 'Across the Barricades'

WRITTEN COMMUNICATION description - notes - essays - careers information

LIBRARY SKILLS

PRESENTATION SKILLS thoughtful organisation of work

SCHEMES OF WORK

Figure 3   SUPPORT

4 Option 3 Science: BASIC SCIENCE G.C.S.E.

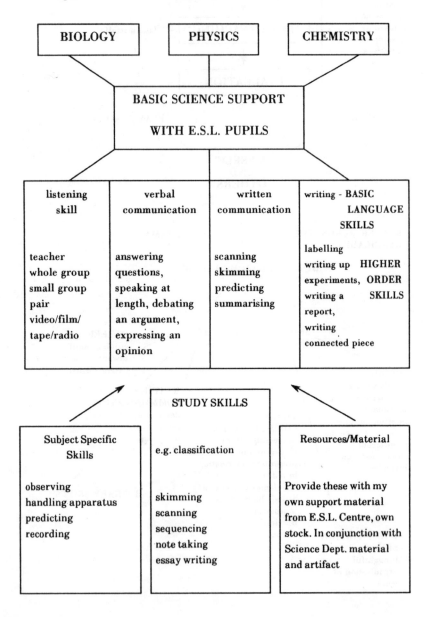

progress, the documents become records of progressive achievement also for their teachers, who are thus enabled to recognise linguistic and cultural strengths which might otherwise be obscured from them in their emphasis on their own professional disciplines.

Agenda for action

It is clear that most secondary schools require an agenda for action whereby they look at an agreed 'language across the curriculum' policy, so that all staff and all departments are responsible for the children's language development and not just the language postholder in the English department and the ESL teachers. All LEAs should declare their commitment to the principles of 'Education for all' - so declared Swann (1985). This needs to be established not only at LEA level but by each individual school.

When such a policy statement has been developed it should include the elements put forward in this paper. Neither the National Curriculum nor indeed the whole of the Education Reform Act (1988) addresses the issue of the needs of bilingual pupils. These should be emphatically highlighted so that the learning environment does justice to a multilingual society. After all, we have had not only Swann (1985) but Bullock (1975) who said:

> *In a linguistically conscious nation in the modern world, we should see it as an asset, as something to be nurtured, and one of the agencies that should nurture it is the school ... the school should adopt a positive attitude towards its pupils' bilingualism and whenever possible should help maintain and deepen their knowledge of their mother tongue.*

That was nearly fifteen years ago. We cannot afford to wait another fifteen years.

Modern languages and the language curriculum: co-operation and diversity

Alan Hornsey

Traditionally, modern foreign languages were taught in schools because they were thought to provide training for the mind, access to a different culture through its literature, insights which could lead to more refined use of English and possible career openings in trade and diplomacy. Recently these four aims have been questioned and gradually replaced by intentions more in line with a wider and more popular concept of educational value. For 'mind training' read communicative skills; for 'literature' the culture of everyday life; for 'more refined use of English' general awareness of language; for 'trade and diplomacy' more humble work possibilities or even holidays. In short, the traditional, somewhat exclusive, reasons for having a modern foreign language on the school timetable have been replaced with elements which, thirteen years ago in 1975, might well have appealed to the members of the Bullock Committee (Bullock, 1975) and given foreign languages a prominent place in the final report.

Parallel to this change in aims has been a change in the profile and aspirations of the foreign-language teachers themselves. Most have laboriously learnt to speak the language they teach; they have studied abroad as part of their degree course (taking five years to train instead of the usual four); they have willingly participated in the everyday lives of the native speakers of the language and they have reduced, without rejecting completely, the influence of bookish approaches to their subject. They have personally gained from a close relationship with our foreign neighbours and they believe that the lives of their pupils could be enriched in the same way. For this reason they devote time to school visits abroad and they try to bring more of the language and the feel of the country into their classrooms. They should certainly not carry all the blame if their efforts are frustrated and bring little reward, for they garden in a gale[1] of English while trying to do oral work with overlarge classes, inadequate timetabling and pupils who very

1. Image taken from Hawkins, E. *Modern languages in the curriculum*, Cambridge University Press (1981).

much reflect an insular view of language as often held by their parents and society in general. It is not an exaggeration to suggest that the new aspirations, as embodied for example in the best of GOML schemes and most of the GCSE criteria, represent a development painfully achieved despite the difficulties. Discussion of modern languages in the curriculum today must rid itself of an out-dated caricature of language teachers as espousing elitist aims and, in any case, not being competent in the language they purport to teach. It will also need to take into account the context in which they are expected to work.

I have deliberately gone over old ground because what I have said about aims and image is an essential background to a crucial issue which has to be faced by language teachers in the late eighties, namely how to respond to linguistic diversity and to the presence in schools of a large number of pupils who regularly speak or hear a range of languages different from our past traditions. They use languages not traditionally encompassed by the subject 'modern languages'. They may even be perceived as a threat to the acquired skills of the teachers in post and to the position of European culture in schools. Worst of all, they can be seen as a problem rather than a possible advantage. After all, those new aims - communication skills, experience of a different culture, awareness of language - are just as likely to accrue from studying Gujarati as German, and if these 'new' languages perhaps lack commercial possibilities or a direct share in our 'Europeanness', they are clearly the languages of close neighbours and fellow-citizens: they will certainly play a part in any coherent language programme alongside English and a European language in a number of schools, especially in certain inner-city areas. In short, they represent a massive resource and they remind us of the very existence of variety.

Coherence will not mean that all language teachers will behave in the same way. There will be a common will to sharpen pupils' language skills and their sensitivity to the ways in which we use language to communicate, but these outcomes will be achieved by teachers doing what their particular subject is best fitted to do. Thus it is neither relevant nor helpful to use emotive concepts like snobbery or imperialism in order to persuade foreign language teachers to espouse the practice of English as a Foreign Language, nor would it be likely that the insights of specialists in linguistics[2] can be immediately converted into a major contribution to modern language methodology. Equally unacceptable is the not uncommon attempt of modern language teachers to blame English teachers for not providing their pupils with the kind of 'dead' grammar mistakenly assumed to be an essential prerequisite for foreign-language learning. What is needed is an elaborated form of Brumfit's charter, a specification of what the language curriculum should provide. The charter would then be analysed in terms of appropriate learning activities and the contributions of various subjects identified. Finally, the time on the timetable would be allocated as appropriate:

> Step 1 Specification of needs
> Step 2 Activities and subjects identified
> Step 3 Appropriate distribution of time

Step 3 will of course be difficult to realise if a powerful agency (a department of education or a secretary of state, for example) simply allocates time in sealed parcels to subject specialists who might follow their traditions regardless of an overall purpose.

I would not wish, as Christopher Brumfit does, to invoke here the concept of 'rights'. Instead, I prefer a humanistic approach to 'needs' by saying that the process of education must stem from answers to the questions 'what does it mean to be an adult human being in our society?' One answer is that our society is language-saturated and that the quality of our participation in it will be enhanced or reduced by the success of the language teaching we receive. We are obviously at a disadvantage if we cannot read and write; we will probably gain by being able to spell and punctuate with reasonable concern for the potential reader, but language teaching must mean much, much more than that. Personal relationships, social life, leisure, business, political participation, even our talk to ourselves and our imagination require a school language policy which provides for:

recognition of variety - spoken/written, standard/dialect, etc
breadth - language of fact, fiction, information, imagination, control, self-expression, etc
skill/tact - ability to fit language to situation

2. e.g. Krashen, S. D. *Second language acquisition and second language learning*, Oxford: Pergamon (1981), p 37.

confidence - to express oneself or to meet new language situations

This is only a start. An agreed specification could be drawn up by linguists like Brumfit together with teachers and members of the community outside the education profession.

When will these languages needs be met? I would hope that English teaching will confront variety, both in terms of language experienced and the kinds of expression the pupils are invited to try. Both here and in any work with linguistic minorities there will presumably be emphasis on effectiveness and on confidence. These qualities will also have their place in every other subject on the curriculum and all of the teachers concerned will be better placed than I am to examine and discuss their particular contribution. Writing as a foreign-language teacher, I can see what the role of that subject has to be:

1. to nurture receptive skills, providing work in precise listening and careful reading;

2. to reveal something of the nature of communication as pupils are called upon to express simple propositions in a new way;

3. to show something (modestly) of the relationship between word, concept and social setting;

4. to suggest that different does not mean worse;

5. to encourage through comparison a review of what is taken for granted in languages which the pupil already knows;

6. to teach something of the metalanguage or terminology of language, what Vigotsky would have called 'scientific concepts';

7. to require pupils to experiment with hypotheses about the new code they are learning - not a long way removed from work in natural sciences or computer studies.

Here I would like to be quite explicit in my rejection of three beliefs which seem to have become associated with modern languages:

1. *Only certain languages matter*

Any natural language could serve my purpose, and the exclusion of languages other than say, French, German or Spanish from serious consideration can only rest on a belief derived from teacher-availability and the proximity of the countries, and not from any inherent virtues.

2. *A teacher can teach any language*

The teacher must be both a skilful user of the language and also know a great deal about its culture. The belief that a teacher can teach any language is erroneous. A lot of problems of language teaching stem from people pretending to teach their subsidiary languages orally or even dabbling in languages they hardly know for the purpose of providing 'taster' courses.

3. *All language taught in the classroom should aim to be communicative*

The slogan 'we now teach French for communication' is dangerously misleading. Secondary school classrooms are just about the worst possible location for such an aim and, in any case, the slogan can easily lead to a phrase-book style of learning, where all the pupil gains is an ill-memorised repertoire which is only superficially language-like.

I hasten to add that I do believe children need to gain the tools of very basic survival in the foreign country, but this alone is hardly a sufficient justification for a key place in the curriculum for five years. The justification is to be found in the combination of my seven roles plus the insights gained into a foreign culture. The modern language is best suited to contributing to, as I have indicated, and complementing thereby the work of English and/or other mother-tongue teachers. All three must as appropriate be included in my timetable.

The timetable I propose was first included in a talk I gave at the ILEA Language Centre in Autumn 1985. The talk was published in abbreviated form in Spring 1986 (Hornsey, 1986)[3]. The starting point is my belief that the successful growth of an

---

3.   Modern and community languages - convergence or divergence? *Bulletin*,
     ILEA Languages Centre, Spring 1986. The plan was then more radical and
     not constrained by National Curriculum proposals.

educated person is bound up with a confident relationship to language and that therefore schools must provide the possibility of investigating one's preferred language or languages, of widening and refining one's language experience and of stimulating awareness of how language operates. The effort to learn a foreign language is an essential ingredient. I have modified my position of 1985[4] in the light of the proposals for a National Curriculum and of HMI guidelines, not because I entirely agree with them but because they look set to become the reality within which language teachers will have to operate. I have already hinted that the subject-based division of the curriculum proposals will not help attempts to form a coherent language policy, and I fear that the policy for diversification (no second foreign language before the fourth form and little encouragement of community languages, for example) will leave French in an even more entrenched position.

I am assuming about nine lessons for English and a foreign language in years 1 to 3 and the possibility of about three more lessons in years 4 and 5 for those who want to pursue another language. The languages chosen will be determined by the school, its traditions, its location and the presence or absence of bilingual pupils in substantial numbers.

Years 1, 2, 3

ENGLISH (5 lessons)

Work to include some cross-referencing to the foreign language being taught and to other languages spoken by pupils. Agreed aspects of LANGUAGE AWARENESS to be covered.

FOREIGN LANGUAGE (4 lessons)

A course to include skill acquisition, some attention to form and structure, comparison with mother tongues.

LANGUAGE AWARENESS

The work in language awareness should not be seen as separate

---

4. My plan at that time was as outlined on p 60.

but should arise as appropriate. There will be a checklist rather than a syllabus which will include:

- talk about language in general - what it is, how it works, what it does;

- comparisons between languages, using those known by teachers and pupils as a resource. For example, forms of address (different pronouns meaning you), words used regularly in expressing family relationships, examples of different word order could be discussed. Advertisements taken from popular magazines and newspapers can give rise to talk about style, and comparisons in different languages will show how resources in these are used differently;

- the learning of the basic greetings and politenesses, numbers, ways of telling the time, etc in several languages. This should not be a pretence that the languages are being 'learnt' but should be a sampling activity giving modest experience of what is involved in learning a language;

- the telling and reading in English of some popular stories taken from different language cultures;

- perhaps an introduction to some language terminology and to the intelligent use of dictionaries.

Years 4, 5

ENGLISH (4 lessons)

Work as appropriate towards General Certificate of Secondary Education (GCSE)

FOREIGN LANGUAGE (4 lessons)

Work as appropriate towards GCSE

ANOTHER LANGUAGE (4 lessons)

This could be one of the languages currently available OR one of the community languages as a language already spoken or as a new foreign language.

The constraints of the National Curriculum and HMI guidelines are painfully clear and my proposals now look rather conservative. My intention is to encourage a modest beginning of co-operation across the language fields, to provide a role for other languages in the language awareness work which can be built on in years 4 and 5 and to create an awareness of language which will enrich and accelerate the learning of a further language so late in the course. Without this awareness and if the options set against the language are too important to miss, my fear of an increased hegemony of French will be justified. Positive steps must be taken, otherwise only children whose schools are not bound by the national rules will be able to benefit from a policy designed to help them become full linguistic participants in the adult world. English, foreign-language and community-language teachers will have to get together.

	3 lessons	6 lessons	
YEARS 1 & 2	LANGUAGE (AWARENESS) Differences, forms, use. Greetings and politenesses in several languages - use of languages known to teacher and pupils	ENGLISH (with intensive ESL/EFL as required)	
	3 lessons (A)	3 lessons (B)	3 lessons (C)
YEARS 3, 4 and 5 (English or ESL **must** be chosen)	1 from: Community lang. 1. Community lang. 2. German French English	1 from: Comm. lang. 1/SL Comm. lang. 2/SL German French Spanish English	1 from: Lang & Communication Spanish ESL English

EXAMPLES: Years 3-5

Pupil		Home Language	Choice	Groups
Pupil	1	English	F G E	A B C
	2	English	Sp Lang & Comm E	B C A
	3	English	G Lang & Comm E	B C A
	4	English	F Beng 2 E	A B C
	5	Greek	F G E	A B C
	6	Bengali	G Beng 1 ESL	B A C
	7	Bengali	F Lang & Comm E	B A C
	8	Greek	F Greek 1 ESL	B A C
	9	English	F Sp E	A B C
	10	Bengali	Lang & Comm Beng E	C A B
	11	Bengali	F Sp E	A B C
	12	Bengali/Gujarati	F Beng 2 ESL	A B C

British languages

Bryden Keenan

Raising the temperature of debate

In a *Times Educational Supplement* review on 29 January 1988, Mahendra Verma referred to *the current lukewarm debate on the theme of societal bi-multilingualism (SIC), in Britain.*[1] This contribution will attempt to raise the temperature a little and turn up the lights, mainly with reference to curriculum provision for community languages, and in wholehearted endorsement of Michael Marland's forthright and perceptive view, as expressed in his book *Multilingual Britain* (Marland, 1987), that we are talking about *one of the greatest changes in British life - the move to a multilingual society.*

Lukewarm is certainly the impression given by the Swann Report (Swann, 1985). It is far from being lukewarm throughout, but the hot and cold tend to neutralise each other. Both elements are present in the first paragraph of the chapter on *Language and language education*:

> *The English language is a central unifying factor in 'being British', and is the key to participation on equal terms as a full member of this society. There is, however, a great diversity of other languages spoken amongst British families in British homes ... In order to lay the foundations for a genuinely pluralist society the education system must, we believe, both cater for the linguistic needs of ethnic minority pupils and also take full advantage of the opportunities offered for the education of all pupils by the linguistic diversity of our society today. To avoid misunderstandings, it should be said straightaway that this does not, as will become apparent, mean the teaching of school subjects in languages other than English, save for one area, the modern languages curriculum.*

Some have objected to the description of the English language as a unifying factor, but this is surely a true picture of the position. However, the fine words about a pluralist society and catering for the linguistic needs of ethnic minority pupils are neutralised

1. 'Recipe for a bilingual society'. *TES*, 29 January 1988, p 27.

by the negative remarks at the end. Those who disagree with the final sentence quoted will find it a nice irony that it is written in faulty English! This question is pursued under the heading of 'Curriculum Provision'.

National Curriculum policy

Since there is so little agreement generally about policy for community languages, it is understandable that the DES and HMI have been reluctant to go into print on the subject. In 1983 HMI did review mother tongue teaching in four LEAs (HMI, 1984). Generally, their report is a neutral document, but it does have some praise for ILEA policies and for some good primary practice:

> *In some of the work seen there is evidence of direct benefit to the pupils in responding to their first language. This is particularly the case in some first and infants' schools where a carefully planned approach has enabled pupils to engage more fully with normal school work.*

In the Consultative Paper *Foreign Languages in the School Curriculum* (DES, 1983), the DES simply made a position statement and asked a few questions. It did, however, acknowledge the importance of the wishes of the local communities and the factor of availability of staff and resources.

In 1987 the Curriculum Matters 8 HMI Paper *Modern Foreign Languages to 16* (HMI, 1987) went further and devoted five paragraphs to languages of ethnic minority communities. Unfortunately, the section had all the signs of a hasty, poorly written afterthought and did not advance the debate.

The National Curriculum draft published in July 1987 (DES, 1987) does not address the question at all, but it does speak of accommodating *the distinctive needs of the Welsh curriculum* (Annex A), and makes a statement about the 'Special Position of Welsh' (paragraph 19):

> *The Welsh language is a part of the curriculum of most children in Wales. The Government's policy is that some experience of the language is an important component of a broadly balanced curriculum for pupils in Wales: that in English-speaking areas all pupils should be given the opportunity of acquiring a sufficient command of Welsh to*

allow for communication in Welsh, while bilingual education
should be available to pupils whose parents desire it for
them.

It is difficult to construct an argument for treating Urdu,
Bengali, Panjabi, Turkish, Greek, etc any differently in certain
parts of the country. There must be official recognition that
these languages are here to stay for a very long time and that in
certain urban areas they are much more widely spoken than
Welsh in any part of Wales. Surely it is not enough to say that
Welsh has been here much longer than the other languages
mentioned or that the Bible was translated into Welsh 400 years
ago. There is no real argument against rewording paragraph 23
of the national policy statement *Modern Languages in the School
Curriculum* (1988) to read:

> *We see no reason for different policies in Tower Hamlets and
> Wales. In Tower Hamlets the Bengali language has a place
> in the curriculum, though the extent of Bengali language
> teaching varies. Bengali is also employed as a medium of
> instruction in many other subjects. Pupils who are learning
> Bengali should also have the opportunity to study one and,
> for those able to benefit, two modern foreign languages.*

Teachers wishing to teach in Wales or Ireland are required to
have some knowledge of Welsh or Gaelic. Is it therefore
unreasonable to suggest that teachers taking up posts in certain
urban areas should either be able to speak the languages
significantly represented in the schools or should be ready to
attend locally based introductory language courses? Similar
courses might be provided in Creole language awareness and be
just as vital in widening awareness of the local communities'
needs.

Curriculum provision

The most common way of introducing community languages into
mainstream secondary school provision is at fourth year level.
From an organisational point of view this is very
understandable. There is no need to worry about which subjects
will have to lose time to accommodate the new subject; it is
much easier to timetable a peripatetic teacher into the 70-minute
periods which are more common in the fourth year than in

earlier years. And yet this administrative convenience cannot obscure the fundamental illogicality of the Swann Report's attempt to keep community languages out of the curriculum of children between the ages of seven and fourteen.

The *Bedford Mother Tongue and Culture Project* (1976-80), the *Bradford MOTET (Mother Tongue and English Teaching) Project* (1978-80) and the *Linguistic Minorities Project* (1979-83) have all concluded that if part of the primary curriculum is conducted through the medium of the mother tongue, there are benefits for English, as well as the obvious gains in children's confidence and in home-school liaison. In spite of pious expressions of the need to concentrate on English, nobody has come up with irrefutable evidence to suggest that mother tongue teaching impedes progress in English. Strategies for supporting bilingual students have been very well outlined by Silvaine Wiles in the relevant chapter of 'Language and Learning: an interactional perspective' (Wells and Nicholls, 1985). Ethnic minority communities are warning that there is an increasing danger of children arriving at the age of fourteen completely illiterate in their mother tongues and therefore needing more than a two-year course even to reach the level of GCSE. This is a wasteful procedure. It would be better for children to study their own languages at eleven instead of the first foreign language. It might be a matter of some concern that they would be the only group of children not studying a foreign language, but they would be able to take up a foreign language at the stage at which other children are offered a second foreign language. Pupils who are proficient enough to sit GCSE early might even be able to take up two other languages before the age of sixteen. This scheme would not of course be possible if, as is rumoured, the National Curriculum[2] is going to specify certain languages as appropriate for first foreign language status and others not: North Asian languages yes, South Asian no. The idea seems preposterous.

Another alternative might be for a school to take advantage of the expertise of a particular teacher to offer one or two other curriculum subjects through the medium of a mother tongue. When such experiments are carried out through the medium of a foreign European language, they attract interest and praise, and nobody ever asks if the pupils will be handicapped when they

2. *Ed. Note:* See the Education (National Curriculum) (Modern Foreign Language) Order 1989 and Afterword (this volume).

come to take public examinations in these subjects in English. In spite of the Swann Report's objections, quoted at the beginning of this chapter, such initiatives must be worth pursuing in community languages.

In determining the place of community languages in the curriculum, it is as well to heed the warning of the *Linguistic Minorities Project report* 'The Other Languages of England' (LMP, 1985, page 377):

> *Most of the world's population, and its school systems, are bilingual or multilingual... . The learning of a second language is helped by building a strong foundation in the first. Bilinguals have the potential for developing specific cognitive and social skills. But in Europe at least these are much more often exploited by upper- and middle-class people. And in most parts of the world bilingualism is all too often valued only with reference to high-status languages. When bilinguals belong to the subordinate sections, and there is an imbalance between the status of their two languages, their potential linguistic skills are often lost and their bilingualism is defined as - and thus becomes - problematic. The bilingual skills of this latter group are rarely acknowledged in the official criteria of achievement established in, for example, school curricula or public language examinations.*

The Italian lesson

In Italy, dialects are still widely spoken but people are increasingly likely to be either completely bilingual with Italian or at least fully able to understand standard Italian. Children born in this country to families of Italian origin may have no exposure at all to speakers of standard Italian. Moreover, there are more and more mixed marriages in which children are brought up speaking English only. This in no way removes the urgent social need for these children to be able to communicate with their families in Italy.

A Bedford school has for some years had some 25 children of Italian background in each year-group who have chosen to study Italian instead of a second foreign language and who have been taught by Italian Consulate teachers, the Italian Government's own version of Section 11 (see glossary).

After some years of Italian exclusively for Italians, the logical step was taken of bringing in Italian as an alternative second foreign language for all. A British-trained teacher was appointed. This move has been most successfully developed and there is now co-operation between the two kinds of classes. At the moment they are still taught separately, but as the Italian-Italian groups become less and less automatically bilingual, the day cannot be far distant when the classes will be 'mixed', at least from the second year of study onwards. This will of course create a problem over who should teach the group - a problem that is familiar to those who struggle with Section 11 regulations. The point is that, just as the definition of a child as 'bilingual Italian' is becoming less and less clear cut, the same will happen eventually with children of Asian background.

GCSE criteria for community languages

First reactions to the adoption of the French criteria for community languages have predictably and understandably been indignant. There were similar reactions to the Swann Report's call for community languages to be seen as part of the modern languages department, with the implication that these languages were foreign. Yet each move is towards higher status and recognition and should be welcomed as such, even if better things can be hoped for in the future.

Contrary to some predictions, many heads of modern language departments have been very ready to welcome community language teachers and their languages, and have been most conscientious in their support. They have invited them into their classrooms as a prelude to discussion on teaching methods; they are beginning to realise how desirable it is to find teachers who are equipped to teach both a European and an Asian language, rather than to rely on part-time peripatetic teachers. Surely this is far better than having community languages seen as part of ESL or even of remedial provision!

Similarly, those who reject the criteria adopted for community languages at GCSE must be forgetting how severely inappropriate community language 'O' level papers were. Only four years ago, a London 'O' level Urdu examiner was allowed to ask candidates to write 170 words on 'The Arabs' - yes, 'O' level! The prose translations have been of a level which would have defeated 'A' level candidates in European languages. Preparations for GCSE in community languages have been even more rushed than for European languages and there will be much room for improvement, but at least these papers will give teachers every incentive to teach genuine and useful communication skills. There will also be an incentive to teach about the countries of origin and their culture. It is to be hoped that this will bring about improvements in the quality and quantity of teaching materials. Many objections to the new syllabuses seem to be saying no more than that they are too easy and therefore lower the status. If the papers were becoming easier than for European languages one could understand the objection, but they are not. A comparable level of attainment is being set. If bilingual children can pass this level earlier or much earlier than others, that is appropriate and right. They will then be able to move on to 'A' level or the Bilingual Skills Certificate of the Royal Society of Arts, or simply make room in their timetables for another subject. Italian children in Bedford have never objected that the French-style Italian 'O' level was too easy for them; on the other hand, no one has ever attempted to make provision for them to take all other papers in specially prepared mother tongue versions.

Section 11 staffing for community languages

The deployment of almost all staff who have used and developed a knowledge of community languages in secondary schools has been directed towards the needs of children of Commonwealth origin, and consequently has legitimately used funds made available under Section 11 of the 1966 Local Government Act. This has enabled LEAs to make a flexible response to schools' requests and has meant that classes have been able to start without the minimum of fifteen that a school's staffing would normally dictate. Sometimes classes have only become viable after the start of the September term, as news of the class spread only slowly through school and community. This is excellent use of Section 11 provision (see glossary) and it is difficult to see how else the particular needs of bilingual children could have been catered for. Where numbers remain small in a school, there will be a continuing need for subsidised help, probably from a peripatetic team. However, if classes move into a viability which is likely to continue, it is not reasonable for a school to evade making permanent provision. It is to be hoped that the initiatives taken by schools to place their own teachers on establishment can complement continuing Home Office funding for teachers under Section 11, even if this funding is likely to be reduced progressively over a period of years. In this way the Home Office can continue to encourage good practice. If funding is simply refused for all new applications and applications for renewal are abruptly reduced from 75% to nothing, many of the gains of the last few years will disappear.

Terminology

In such sensitive areas as multicultural education, anti-racism and community languages, it is both important and difficult to find expressions which will offend no one. For example, 'black people' can safely be used in a variety of contexts, but 'blacks' cannot. The Swann Report had a particular purpose when it entitled one of its chapters 'Liverpool blacks'. 'Indigenous' is an increasingly problematic word. It is often used to mean 'white', which it does not, or 'English-speaking', which it does not. There does not in fact seem to be any single word for white people born in this country speaking only English and having no foreign blood imports since William the Conqueror. Rather than bewail this unfortunate gap in the English language, perhaps we should see it as a conscious blank for something that we do not need. Mother tongues are called various things, including heritage and community languages. The *Linguistic Minorities Project* called these languages 'the other languages of England'. David Houlton's practical celebration of linguistic diversity in primary schools called them 'All our languages' (Houlton, 1985). Perhaps it is even more appropriate to call them what they have now become: BRITISH LANGUAGES.

CASE STUDIES

It is difficult to generalise about the experiences of bilingual pupils, given the wide divergence both in terms of their linguistic loyalties, and also in terms of the differential responses of different schools. It is easier to generalise about the education system and its perceptions of bilingual children. The case studies in this section are preceded by Laurie Kershook's general review of the educational context within which teachers and pupils operate. The studies themselves illustrate the differing specific demands made on the system by different linguistic communities.

Bilingual pupils: classroom chameleons or the spots on the leopard?

Laurie Kershook

If we accept within the term 'bilingual' any pupil who uses a language other than English - whether actively or passively - on a regular basis, it may be useful to divide bilingual pupils into two groups, whom we could call the 'high profile' and 'low profile' bilinguals. The differentiation refers to the fact that there is one category of bilingual pupils who manage their bilingualism well, and consequently whose presence teachers have tended to ignore, and a second category of obvious under-achievers who have tended to remain at the centre of educational debate, and provide a catalyst for change, as teachers attempt to meet the challenge.

Low profile bilinguals: the classroom chameleons

These are pupils who are sufficiently proficient in the English language to be considered 'English speaking' by their teachers.

They will usually be the children or even the grandchildren of new settlers from outside Britain. They may, however, have been born abroad and have come to England at a very early age.

A mother tongue other than English is likely to be used in their homes. Their knowledge of this mother tongue may range from near perfect to vestigial; the mother tongue itself may be a non-standard variant, spoken within the family or community in a London variant, or within a framework of diglossia or code-switching. The low profile bilingual's ethnic origin will have an important cultural influence on him/her, but not necessarily a positive one. She will not wish to feel 'Greek', or 'Turkish', or

71

'Cypriot,' or 'Mauritian' because that would mean to feel
different or 'foreign'. But she has difficulty in thinking of herself
as 'English' as the cultural influence of 'home' is still strong in
her life. When she returns 'home' to Cyprus or Mauritius, her
use of the mother tongue identifies her as 'English'. But in
England the cultural differences are emphasised in the opposite
direction; she feels 'foreign'.

The parents of the low profile bilingual may themselves value
the retention of the mother tongue. They may use it as the first
or only language of the home, provide books in mother tongue
and encourage the further study of mother tongue at a
community supplementary school. They may be sufficiently at
ease with their biculturalism to foster the concept of 'hyphenated
affiliation', i.e. to feel secure in being Anglo-Cypriot, Anglo-
Bengali, etc. Their children, however, who have less powerful
links with 'home', may find this balanced affiliation difficult to
achieve, and may express a lack of interest in, or even hostility
to, their linguistic origins. This fact is sometimes offered as proof
that bilingualism is a first generation 'problem', cured by the
passing of time and the process of assimilation.

Other bilingual parents may have examined the messages
transmitted by society and concluded that they can best serve
their children's interests by helping them to assimilate into the
dominant culture. They may restrict the use of the mother
tongue to the absolute minimum, encouraging their children to
reject the language and culture of 'home' in favour of that of the
'host' society. Such parents are, in effect, encouraging their
children to hold them and themselves in contempt.

Some parents may discourage the use of mother tongue
because they are conscious that within their own society the
variant of the language they speak may be held in low esteem;
for instance, the Cypriot forms of Greek and Turkish, or the
Sylheti variant of Bengali. Speakers of Mauritian Creole may
refer to it as 'broken French', while most forms of Caribbean
Pa'twa are falsely considered by many not to be languages at all,
but corrupt dialects or 'pidgins' of English.

All these kinds of 'low profile' bilingual have one thing in
common: they have a sufficient grasp of the English language to
appear to be monolingual and many prefer to appear to be so.

Having received sufficient messages, whether implicit or
explicit, from school and society, many pupils conclude, if
perhaps in a subconscious or unarticulated manner, that their
bilingual-bicultural skills are not recognised, understood or

valued. They may view their skills and experience as deviant, even perhaps shameful, at best something in which their teacher should have no interest. In some cases, this view may be supported in the home, in others we, the teachers, are definitely to blame. In an education system which prides itself on being responsible for the care of the whole child, and which boasts an extensive system of pastoral care, we remain too content to define children's needs in terms of problems, and as such to perceive no need where we perceive no problem. The low profile bilingual is able to camouflage him/herself, so as to present no problem to the teacher. If we are content to allow this to happen, we are simply failing in our responsibility to the child, by allowing problems of identity to go unresolved, thereby restricting affective growth and development.

We are neglecting opportunities for showing the bilingual pupil how to make positive use of his/her extended repertoire of language to enrich and enhance his/her learning experience.

We are missing opportunities to initiate valuable exchanges of expertise among pupils which validate all cultures and all forms of knowledge, and which use the pupils' own experience as the starting point of learning.

We are missing the opportunity to show that we value all languages and all cultures, and thus to inject an important antiracist element into the curriculum.

We are allowing an important element of the child's educational experience to go unacknowledged by us, especially if the pupil attends a community supplementary school, as so many do.

Only when the classroom teacher - whatever her subject specialism - has come to understand the value of bilingualism as a resource for learning and has equipped herself with the knowledge, the skills and the strategies necessary to harness that resource, will the 'low profile' bilingual be prepared to reassert skills and build on them.

High profile bilinguals: catalysts for change

For the 'high profile' bilingual pupil there is no possibility of camouflage in a context of monolingual norms. In contrast to low profile bilinguals who, in expressing no easily recognisable need, communicate no immediate problem, high profile bilinguals present a real and pressing problem to the teacher: lack of

English means that even basic transactional communication is virtually impossible.

These are the Beginner Bilinguals, pupils who, newly arrived in England, are highly conspicuous in classrooms, so conspicuous that they actually expose the inadequacies of the education system. In addition to speaking no English, they are likely to be completely unfamiliar with even the rudiments of the intricate, often eccentric, web of rules, methods and conventions which characterise British secondary education. They may, indeed, be total strangers to British society in any form.

Despite much discussion in recent years about education issues **across** the curriculum, secondary education remains tied to a hierarchy and organisation rooted in subject specialism. The public examination system with its emphasis on the acquisition of selected bodies of knowledge is a major factor in the retention of this artificial constraint. The secondary school teacher, therefore, is subject to certain specific pressures: she has an obligation to impart to her pupils the body of knowledge which constitutes the syllabus content, but the needs of the eleven-year-old pupil newly arrived in England and speaking no English differ considerably from those of a fourteen-year-old counterpart.

It is highly probable that the high profile bilingual will be found in an inner city school, in a classroom where the pupils represent a wide continuum of social and educational need. In attempting to prioritise those needs and decide on strategies for action without adequate support, the teacher may mistakenly take the view that there is no point in the pupil attending the lesson, since much of it will be incomprehensible and the pupil is learning nothing of either the English language or the subject matter. The teacher may well take refuge in the belief that the good of the greatest number will be achieved if the high profile bilingual is removed to some kind of reception class or unit and given a rudimentary course in English, after which she can return to the subject specialist classroom better equipped to participate and benefit. Other colleagues may express the view that such strategies are negative, divisive and perhaps even harmful to Beginner Bilinguals.

In the meantime, needing to cope despite the subject teacher's increasing sense of inadequacy, the high profile bilingual develops a strategy of being as inconspicuous as possible; in effect, she lowers her profile, and learns to be less demanding. In a school which has developed effective support systems for Beginner Bilinguals, this tendency will be noted and checked; where no systems or policies exist, and the pressures on individual teachers are consequently excessive, such a tendency is likely to go unchecked.

Conclusion

High profile bilinguals continue and will continue to present teachers with needs which must be understood and met, if the classroom is not to cease functioning as a means of effective education. Their presence in a school in significant numbers therefore stimulates intensive curriculum debate.

Low profile bilinguals do not stimulate anything like the same level of debate. Nevertheless, analysis of the needs of low and high profile bilinguals shows us that their needs, once acknowledged, are not significantly different. This suggests that a main task in future should be to focus attention on the proficient user of English who through family or community circumstances is potentially bilingual.

This should bring about a reappraisal of organisation, methodologies, materials and assessment procedures, and thus an enhanced understanding of the educational needs of all pupils.

Educational problems of Chinese children in British schools

Lornita Yuen-Fan Wong

Chinese pupils in Britain can be broadly divided into two main groups based on their country of birth - those born in Britain and the immigrants. Since the majority of children from both groups has been educated according to Chinese values and using the Chinese language within the family environment, the problems they face in British schools seem quite similar in some respects. Their specific problems in British schools fall into two main categories: the first relating to achievement in the mainstream curriculum and the second to the maintenance of Chinese identity and cultural values.

Achievement in the mainstream curriculum

According to figures compiled by the DES, about 70 per cent of the Chinese pupils in British schools speak Cantonese and 25 per cent speak Hakka as their home language. Among the Chinese in Britain, it is estimated that about 65 to 75 per cent of first generation Chinese are unable to speak English (Great Britain, 1985). In other words, before Chinese children go to British schools, the majority of them are brought up in a Chinese family where they learn to speak Chinese for at least four or five years.

Many Chinese children have language problems when they begin schooling in Britain, and have difficulty in following classroom instructions. Some of them retreat into what has been described as 'silent misery'.

The English language problems confronting older Chinese pupils, especially immigrant children, are probably more serious, since these children come to Britain between the ages of eight and sixteen, having had at least two years of education in Hong Kong where schooling begins at six and the medium of instruction in most of the primary schools is Cantonese. Since, in Britain, school starts at five, in reality such a gap can be larger and is exacerbated by the fact that the language of instruction is English. When immigrant children continue their schooling in Britain, they are usually placed at a level according to their age. In theory, immigrant children from Hong Kong will miss at least a year of education when they are placed in the British education system.

Lai Ying was a sixteen-year-old Chinese girl (newly arrived in Britain at the age of twelve). Before Lai Ying left Hong Kong, she had not yet completed primary 5. After being placed in a language centre to learn English for three months, she was allocated to a class in the second year of a secondary school. It is obvious that the girl had 'missed' two years of schooling. The missing years are critical because they are the time when learning becomes more serious and new concepts are introduced. In other words, the content of education becomes more difficult. It is not unusual for English-speaking children to face problems in learning at this stage of schooling even though they are learning through their mother tongue. What happens to children if they are pushed up two years, not because of their outstanding ability, but because of age, and at the same time are using a new language which they have only been exposed to for a couple of months? Underachievement or failure in the system? What happened to Lai Ying was that she skipped classes quite often, and eventually dropped out of school without the knowledge of her family.

Maintenance of Chinese identity and cultural values

Chinese parents in Britain want their children to succeed in education and also to maintain their cultural identity - to be able to communicate with them in Chinese and accord them respect. But in Britain, Chinese children are confronted with two sets of apparently incompatible values which give rise to cultural conflicts.

In spite of a lack of understanding and sympathy in school for Chinese culture, evidence from interviews with students at a Chinese supplementary school suggests that most are quite positive about their own cultural identity and supportive of their own language. Various powerful external forces, however, such as the pervasive influence of English in school, and at home through the mass media, might be expected to weaken their allegiance to their cultural and linguistic roots.

Without understanding the social pressures, some Chinese parents and the Chinese community complain that the next generation in Britain have lost their cultural identity or have forgotten their roots simply on the basis of not speaking the

Chinese language at home (Griffiths, 1982; National Children's Centre, 1984).

When Chinese children go to school in Britain, they are taught Western values which may be in conflict with those Chinese traditional values maintained by some of the Chinese parents in Britain. At home, some of these Western cultural values acquired by Chinese children will unconsciously be exhibited. Some of these children think their parents are too authoritarian. Conservative Chinese parents, in turn, interpret such a challenge from their children as a lack of respect and blame the British education system for inculcating 'barbarian' ideas into their children.

In fact, the conflict in the relationship between Chinese parents and their children does not simply arise from the different values inculcated into the Chinese children at British schools. The traditional practice of sending children back to Hong Kong to be brought up by their grandparents is one of the major factors here.

Chinese children conscious of maintaining their cultural identity are often seen by mainstream school teachers as reluctant to mix with other children at school (Quaker Community Relations Committee, 1981). The examples below, based on interviews and case studies, attempt to explain Chinese children's reticent attitude towards integration with the majority students.

CASE 1

Kwok Wah, an eight-year-old British born Chinese boy was observed by the author for more than a year. According to assessment reports from his school and an educational psychologist, the boy's performance in school was not satisfactory, and his verbal communication skills at six years and nine months old were below average. His teachers saw him as a 'passive, withdrawn' child with moderate learning difficulties who should be sent to a special school. When the child was observed in a classroom situation at the mainstream school, he sat quietly at the back of the classroom and seemed not to be concentrating. When the child's withdrawn behaviour was checked with the teachers at his Chinese school, the teachers there saw nothing strange as there were a couple of other students in the same class who were as quiet as he was. The class teacher of the child even emphasised that he would see these children as 'introverts' but that they are normal.

Other observations showed that the child was not in fact as quiet or anti-social as the mainstream school teachers imagined, but could be as naughty, lively and sociable as other children. At his eighth birthday party at home, for example, he ate, sang and played with other children among whom there were four Indian/Pakistani neighbours and one British girl who is his sister's friend.

From observation and from what the older sister said, the three children of the family were revealed to be the only Chinese at the school; they had suffered from bullying. The boy's 'withdrawn' attitude resulted from a sense of insecurity and a desire to avoid trouble.

Studies in integration

These are studies of the degree of integration of four examples of teenage Chinese children with the majority pupils, based on two secondary schools and a Chinese community centre.

EXAMPLE 1

A group of students was observed in an after-school Chinese class at one of the two schools where the author was the teacher. There were in total five pupils (two Chinese immigrant girls and three British girls without any Chinese background) in the class. Though the class was small, it had divided itself into two non-interacting racial sectors, with the British sitting together separately from the Chinese. Despite the fact that four of the girls were in their fifth year, they seldom had verbal exchanges with one another except on some occasions when they were asked to explain one another's festivals or languages. Sometimes when their 'partners' were absent, they still preferred to remain in their usual seats. Later in the year one of the Chinese girls dropped out from the school. The other Chinese girl simply remained in her own 'camp' alone until the Chinese class was dissolved in April 1987.

From classroom observation and talking with pupils in the two sectors separately on informal occasions, it emerged that the girls had no conflicts at all, and stayed separate mainly because both groups were quite reserved and lacked exposure to people from other cultures. They did not quite understand the expectations, areas of interest and values of one another. They needed someone able to focus their attention on issues which could be of interest to both groups, so that they could really work together and begin to share one another's knowledge.

EXAMPLE 2

A second group consisted of three British-born Chinese girls who were in the fourth year in 1986-87 in one school.

Since the three girls were born and had all had their education in Britain, none of them had any problems with spoken English. However, according to the ESL teacher, they seldom mixed with other children and always stayed with one another as a group at school. The girls explained that even though they could speak the language of the majority of their peers, they felt some differences between the school-mates of other races and Chinese friends when they got together. They were quite happy to be in their own Chinese group at school even though there were only three of them. Although these girls seemed to be quite conscious of their own identity in terms of not being very well integrated with other children at school, they did not feel the need to attend supplementary Chinese classes.

EXAMPLE 3

A third group was composed of eight immigrant and British-born Chinese secondary school boys and girls. The major distinguishing feature here is that these children went to the Chinese community centre regularly after school, mainly for socialising - chatting, playing games, watching Chinese videos, etc.

When these children were asked whether they went out with non-Chinese friends or had close friends at school who were non-Chinese, none of them did. They explained that they could study with the majority students and talked to them at school but preferred to be close to Chinese friends with whom they could really share their emotions even though they spoke to one another in English.

The conclusion to be drawn from the second and third groups of subjects is that these teenage Chinese children have developed a fairly strong sense of their own cultural identity, not in terms of the maintenance of their mother tongue but in terms of wanting to be close to children of their own race and culture in their social life. Their integration with the majority pupils seems to be confined to studies in the school environment only. Their participation in mainstream schools or integration with the dominant group is quite selective. They only want to take advantage of the British system in order to obtain school credentials for employment in the future but reject full assimilation into British culture. Unfortunately, the Chinese children's behaviour seems not very much appreciated in the British system and is usually interpreted by mainstream school teachers as 'withdrawn', 'unsociable' and 'quiet', reflecting stereotypical emotional problems ascribed to Chinese children in this country.

EXAMPLE 4

The experience of Hoi Yee highlights other typical difficulties faced by Chinese children whom the author sees as having integration problems. Hoi Yee was thirteen/fourteen years old and was studying in the third year in a secondary school.

She joined the school in the first year after she had completed primary 4 in Hong Kong. Having missed some levels of schooling because of immigration, the girl had had to struggle very hard with the language as well as with the content of her studies, and still had fairly serious problems with the English language, despite one-to-one teaching given by a native speaker of English.

Because of her difficulties with English she had formed no relationships within the class, nor had she been close to any of the thirty Chinese children in the school that year, since the girl felt that what she needed was English, not Chinese. Also, she had to help to look after her sister's baby and do housework after school.

Actually, the girl was quite conscientious, as most of her teachers agreed. However, her language barrier, together with the lack of appropriate support and guidance from the family and school, led to her problems of integration and achievement.

The integration problem of this immigrant girl was slightly different from those of the other groups, as it was not so much related to cultural identity as language. Her failure to integrate may be seen as involuntary, too, because, apart from the language barrier, there were some other constraints such as family obligations which did not allow her to spend time with other children after school. Integration with the Chinese children in that school, many of them fluent in spoken English, would have improved her English faster.

Conclusion

Chinese children in British schools are generally seen as hardworking and quiet students. The case studies indicate that as with other ethnic minority groups, there are Chinese underachievers at school who are handicapped by inadequate English language skills and who may not be provided with the appropriate support service(s). At all levels of the British education system, there are pathetically few teachers of Chinese origin to whom these pupils could relate more satisfactorily.

Besides the English language, the conflict between the values of the Chinese parents and those of Western society as encountered in Britain also contribute to some underachievement in Chinese children. Anxiety arising from cultural conflicts can be seen in the case studies described above to exercise negative effects on the academic performance of culturally different children.

Chinese community schools, particularly with British mainstream support, could help to solve some of these problems, but lack of finance, trained and qualified teachers, and an appropriate curriculum, make it difficult for classes in both the private and maintained sectors to achieve their objectives. But first, the fundamental need is to understand the situation, before attempting to find and apply solutions.

Language maintenance among children of Italian parentage in mainstream secondary schools in Bedford and London: a pilot study

Bruno Cervi

Introduction

Italian immigrants have always placed great importance upon the perpetuation and development of the Italian language among their community, while still acknowledging the dominant role of English for social integration within Britain. The flourishing of voluntary language maintenance schemes testifies to the concern of the immigrants to play a role in the education of their children, in an attempt to resist total assimilation.

In 1971, the Italian Government passed a law (Legge 3.3: 1971, no. 153) providing for educational assistance to Italian migrants and their relatives in all countries where large-scale immigration of Italians had taken place.

One of its aims was to integrate the education that children of Italian immigrants receive in the host countries with knowledge of the language and culture of the country of origin. This appears to be based on the assumption that the prospective users possess fluency in the national language, a view which does not take account of linguistic diversity within the Italian community. In fact, the dialects spoken in the majority of Italian households in the UK differ from one another and from standard Italian as much as Italian differs from any other neo-Latin language (Lepschy and Lepschy, 1977), and limited competence in Italian makes it impossible to follow the syllabus provided for the *corsi integravi di lingua e cultura italiana*, as it is based on a norm which is too close to the norm of the monolingual Italian student in Italy.

The easy option taken by the teachers concerned was that of going to the opposite extreme and teaching Italian as a foreign language. The foreign language approach was reinforced by the interest shown by Italian students in entering for public examinations, and the availability of purpose-designed material and methodological guidelines.

In the wake of the debate stimulated by the EEC directive

486/77 on the education of migrant children, the Italian authorities sought to integrate the provision offered by *Legge 153* into mainstream schools. Whilst the response of primary schools was limited, a number of secondary schools were willing to accept the offer of a teacher from the Italian authorities; Italian was already accepted as a foreign language in the mainstream curriculum, albeit on a small scale.

Difficulties arise when the aim of the teaching is to help pupils of Italian origin to maintain competence in the language: the variety of dialects involved makes it difficult to cater for the different language backgrounds, but in mainstream provision two further limitations arise: the school policy may not allow for necessary syllabus modifications; the presence of pupils of non-Italian origin in the programme increases the pressure to adopt the criteria and methodology of foreign language teaching.

Superficial observation of students of Italian origin learning Italian in mainstream schools suggests a stereotype of completely anglicised second-generation Italian students not strongly motivated to learn the language of the country of origin of their parents, or to pass the language on to their own children. If this were the case, the adoption of a foreign language approach would be to some extent justified. But the stereotype may be just as wrong as the assumption that they are fully competent in Italian. Appropriate educational treatment cannot be offered on the basis of assumptions. Hence the need for investigation.

The sample

88 students of Italian origin, learning Italian in voluntary aided Roman Catholic schools, were surveyed in Bedford and London.

Two age groups were selected: fifth year students, having a long record of formal tuition in Italian and, at the time of the survey, on the threshold of public examinations; and third year students who, while not complete beginners in formal tuition, were reasonably unaffected by examination pressures.

A questionnaire was used to collect the data. The questionnaire was presented in bilingual form, although it was anticipated that the Italian part of it might be redundant for all practical purposes; it covered aspects of attitude and motivation in relation to Italian language learning, language background and patterns of language use (Italian and English) and interaction. 'Dialect' was used to indicate any Italian dialect with which individual subjects might be familiar.

Results

The results below summarise those aspects that provide useful indications for the evaluation of current practice in Italian language maintenance within the mainstream curriculum, and for more effective educational planning.

CHOICE OF LANGUAGE IN ANSWERING THE QUESTIONNAIRE

Of the 88 questionnaires, a majority (45) were filled in on the Italian side. The choice of the Italian version, while not necessarily showing language dominance or competence in Italian, was indicative of a more positive attitude to the Italian language than had been expected.

ATTITUDES AND MOTIVATION TO DEVELOP COMPETENCE IN ITALIAN

Out of the 88 subjects, 74 reported themselves to be studying Italian of their own will; 59 reported genuine interest in learning the language. Parental pressure tended to be effective with younger students.

Although a definite conclusion on this issue can only be drawn after further investigation, which will have to include in the sample still younger students than so far considered, it may be possible to infer from the trend in the age difference that positive feedback of progress in the acquisition of the target language increases desire to learn it and leads to the perception of willingness.

Most of the subjects reported study with a view to taking CSE or 'O' level examinations.

In spite of the fact that for most of them the current home language, or at least the language of interaction with parents, is dialect, nearly half the subjects feel that learning Italian will help them to talk to their parents in their own language. The myth of the 'return to Italy' appears to have been handed down to the new generation of British-born Italians.

EVALUATION OF ITALIAN, DIALECT AND ENGLISH

In the comparative evaluation of Italian, Dialect and English, all the languages scored high, with Italian highest in most measures, although no better than neutral on ease or difficulty. This relatively low score on ease/difficulty is understandable, as Italian is, of the three languages concerned, the least used in their everyday interaction, and one for which school demands the attainment of definite academic standards.

Surprisingly, perhaps, Italian scored higher than English on potency measures. Does the pride that these British-born Italians take in their linguistic and cultural heritage lead them to overlook the fact that English has acquired world-wide recognised socio-historical and economic status? Or is the students' evaluation indicative of a conflict that leads them to prefer English in their interaction as the language that gives them access to social integration and mobility but represents a threat to a deep-seated ethnic identity from which they do not wish to part?

Even the Dialect that these offsprings of Italian immigrants are reluctant to use was awarded an overall higher evaluation than English.

LINGUISTIC HABITS WITHIN THE FAMILY

Dialect is the language of the great majority of Italian households, for parental interaction and parent-child interaction, although there is a certain degree of divergence from the parent's (usually father's) choice in favour of English.

But the interactions with siblings present a radically different picture: very limited use of Italian or Dialect and unequivocal preference for English. It can be reasonably assumed that acceptance of parent's choice of Dialect is enforced by the parent's authority, but it could also be indicative of family cohesion.

This leaves open the question of what the significance is of the preference for English in sibling interaction and what factors are more influential than family cohesion. Tosi (1984) suggests that the linguistic behaviour of second-generation Italians may be the result of personal and emotional conflicts. The highly conservative attitude of the first generation in relation to the habits and values of their original traditions represents a strong pole of attraction for young Italians who, nevertheless, on the other hand also aim towards identification with the culture of the host country.

SOCIAL IDENTITY AND DESIRE FOR LANGUAGE MAINTENANCE

The study also showed that British-born Italians following

mainstream programmes of language maintenance appear to be proud of their ancestral ethnicity. If this were seen as a legacy of inferiority, very few elements would prevent them from disowning it other than their surname, as they are not marked by any definite racial traits, they are fluent in English and are entitled to British citizenship by birth.

It could be argued that such strong ethnic identity may be the peculiarity of those interested in language maintenance but is not widespread among the Italians of the second generation as a whole, and bears little relevance to educational planning for those who have chosen to perpetuate the language, other than to show the beneficial effect of language maintenance on self-identification.

The desire to hand over the linguistic heritage to the next generation is also beyond any expectation that anecdotal observation was able to suggest. The percentage of those not interested in language maintenance in the case of inter-ethnic marriage is negligible (2.28%); the percentage of those who would not be interested in maintaining the language in the event of an inter-ethnic marriage is very small (6.82%) and smaller than the percentage showing lack of interest in handing down the high-prestige and instrumentally valuable English language to their children in case of repatriation (10.23).

LANGUAGE LEARNING HISTORY

Before school, the pupils' linguistic experience, in most cases, consisted mainly of Dialect and Italian. It is interesting to note how a good proportion of parents shifted from Dialect, the usual language of interaction between them, to standard Italian or an approximation to it in the linguistic upbringing of their children. This is consistent with the apparent desire to provide their children with a tool for access to social emancipation in the country of origin.

More than half the pupils, however, claimed to have started nursery school with a good command of spoken English and a further tenth claimed that they possessed good English comprehension ability even though they were poor speakers of that language.

At entry to primary school, most possessed that sort of 'surface' competence for cognitively undemanding tasks which often prevents the diagnosis of a linguistic deficit. Significantly, the figure describing the subjects whose home language as children was English is close to that describing parents' literacy in English.

Practical conclusions

Some implications for educational planning can be derived, however tentatively, from the pilot study.

First, the absolute inadequacy of the foreign language approach for the development of the Italian language among children of Italian immigrants. Had the subjects displayed an orientation to learn Italian for merely instrumental purposes, and had they disowned and by now lost their linguistic heritage, there would be more scope for the adoption of criteria and methodologies characteristic of foreign language teaching. But the picture that emerges is that the children of Italian immigrants attending Italian classes in mainstream secondary schools appear to have taken a conscious decision to develop knowledge of the language of their parental heritage and to be highly motivated to pursue their aim. Their linguistic habits include a great deal of Italian and Dialect and these two languages, however different, are perceived as strongly interrelated and are very positively valued. Italian ethnic identity is vividly felt. They may experience a conflict between the desire to identify with the majority group and the attraction exerted by their cultural heritage, but harmonious identification with both cultures can be achieved only if mastery of both languages conveying the values of these two cultures is achieved.

The design of a course for Italian as a community language in the mainstream secondary curriculum will have to take all this into account, and will have to take the existing language repertoires of the students involved as a starting point. An atmosphere will have to be created where children can develop their communicative competence in the target language by means of positive transfer of their knowledge and experience as Dialect speakers. Encouraging the use of Dialect for meaningful communication in a classroom, where some degree of linguistic diversity is bound to be present, will increase awareness that the development of standard Italian is a pre-condition for membership to a wider group. Creating the need to employ the written modes of communication, moreover, will enhance the motivation to develop the national language, as Dialects do not have a written form and even monolingual speakers of a Dialect will have to resort to their shaky competence in Italian to write a letter to their relatives in Italy.

The perception must be deepened that the development of Italian does not need to be achieved by repudiating Dialect. On the contrary, extending their competence of Dialect along the continuum that has Italian at the other end will provide the young Italians with a richer repertoire of intermediate modes of communication, which will make speech adjustment possible in a variety of communicative contexts. As the aims of a community language course include fostering a sense of loyalty to the cultural as well as linguistic heritage, the selection of content to offer for the development of linguistic objectives will have to include texts offering a realistic view of contemporary Italy and its historic past.

Even the attainment of the skills required by the currently available public examinations for Italian could be usefully integrated into a course designed along these lines, if they are presented as being relevant to the participants' context rather than as hurdles to be overcome in order to gain recognition from an examining body.

REFERENCES

Lepschy, A.L. and Lepschy, G. (1977). *The Italian language today*.
London: Hutchinson.

Tosi, A. (1984). *Immigration and bilingual education*.
Oxford: Pergamon Press,

Urdu provision in secondary schools - a survey of attitudes and aims in one London borough

Stella Lewis

The survey on which this article is based was carried out in 1985-86 to discover why pupils chose to study Urdu, what effects the provision of Urdu had, what problems existed and the attitude of the community and the schools.

Introduction

Informal discussions had given the impression that Urdu teaching increased the self-confidence of the South-Asian pupils involved and helped to break down the prejudices of teachers and the education system against the teaching of community languages in school.

40 pupils taking Urdu, mostly to exam level, were interviewed - 36 of South-Asian origin and four of non-South-Asian origin. All the South-Asian pupils were bilingual, with varying degrees of fluency, and several trilingual. All the Urdu teachers, except one, were of South-Asian origin.

In one Junior High, Urdu was offered in the second and third years as an option with German and Spanish. Every pupil did French. This policy resulted, as hoped, in several non-Asian pupils taking up Urdu.

40 pupils taking Urdu were interviewed and, in addition, 36 taking French and/or German (not Urdu) were given a questionnaire.

23 adults were also interviewed: Urdu teachers, heads of modern languages, acting or deputy heads, the teacher-in-charge of the Multi-cultural Development Centre, race relations adviser, adviser for modern languages, assistant education officer and oganiser of the Ethnic Minorities Language Service.

Additional data was collected: views of some parents of pupils taking Urdu, languages spoken by pupils at home and exam passes since the introduction of the subject into schools.

The pupils' comments, reflecting their personal experience of being a pupil of South-Asian origin, living and maybe born in a London borough, were of particular importance. Unfortunately, the following summary of results can only hint at the variety of responses and at the feeling behind them.

Why take, teach or offer Urdu in Schools?

Contrary to the opinion of some teachers, the survey showed that South-Asian pupils did not choose Urdu 'because their parents tell them to' and/or they found it easy, *It's my own language* was the most frequent single reason; several pupils mentioned feelings of shame at not knowing it.

The biggest category of reasons was 'communication' - writing to grandparents, talking to mothers and Muslims locally, and a few mentioned visiting Pakistan.

'Language qualification' (especially exam pass) was a common reason, although the low currency of Urdu was sometimes mentioned: *I won't do 'A' level: some people don't really accept it as a qualification.*

Only half the pupils thought that taking Urdu might help them to find a job (police, community work, receptionist, social services, etc, but only one listed teacher).

Social reasons included the high status of Urdu, better marriage prospects, learning about the background culture, understanding Indian films and because their friends learnt it.

The non-Asian pupils chose Urdu for the challenge, to talk to South-Asian friends, or for jobs. As one said: *You're more likely to meet Asian people in this country than French, German or Spanish people, so it'll be more useful.*

Almost all the pupils gave more reasons for learning Urdu than did their teachers and other adults who tended to emphasise 'parental influence' and 'friends doing it'.

Adults in general gave many more reasons for offering Urdu than they credited pupils with for considering when choosing it, although the list was substantially the same as the pupils'. In addition, one explained: *The fact that the language is spoken, understood or otherwise used by some 10-15% of the borough population makes it more than an academic exercise.*

On the question of jobs, school attitudes varied: in some, no mention; in others, stressing the low status of an Urdu qualification and the difficulty for Asians when seeking work but *increasingly job advertisements mention competence in community languages.*

Many teachers highlighted the increase in the pupils' self-esteem: *I think it tends to give them an inner strength* and *I'd*

91

say you can see the results of this confidence in most of their lessons, and on the value of Urdu offered to all pupils: *It will help the British become truly multicultural - if they want to.*

The lessons themselves and their effects

Most pupils were satisfied and many enthusiastic about their Urdu lessons. Some had friends who now wanted to take Urdu but *I think there's pressure not to do it.*

Pupils liked their teachers and methods of teaching, but particularly the atmosphere of the classes: *When you walk into the class you're like in your own culture.* Non-Asian pupils also liked the friendly feeling.

About two-thirds of the South-Asian pupils had changed in some way since starting to learn Urdu: *I think I used to be embarrassed about my language but now I'm not.* Half the pupils spoke, read or wrote more Urdu at home, others were more interested in their background culture and the pleasure was obvious: *I used to think Pakistan was like Ethiopia but now I know it's got richness and famous places the same as England. I used to hate the idea of going there but now I want to go at least once, I might even marry there. My mum is so pleased and relieved.*

Most teachers thought there had been positive changes since the introduction of Urdu, especially in the growth in pupils self-esteem, but some were careful to qualify this: *I don't know how much is a result of Urdu and how much a result of having spent longer in the country than their older sisters....*

Many felt that the status of the classes and tolerance of staff had also grown: *... now it's well-established and respected and the pupils get good results because they work hard and feel good....* Also *... a few teachers are now thinking of learning some Urdu.*

On the negative side, some staff commented on growing behaviour problems in South-Asian pupils and one put this partly down to the Urdu classes.

Non-South Asians and Urdu

In general, the perceived attitudes of pupils not taking Urdu by those who were taking it were depressingly negative: *Most think it's stupid ... they say things like ... it's an English country so English should be taught* or *... it's not really considered as a* *modern language.* Only one pupil used the word 'racist' but others clearly recognised this element. Non-Asian pupils reported mixed attitudes.

Some South-Asian pupils - in schools where it did not happen - expressed surprise or amusement at the idea of non-Asians learning Urdu, but the great majority felt it would be good: for non-Asians - travel or work in Pakistan or India; for South-Asians - status of language and people; and for both - *we can all get on better.* As for teachers, pupils taking Urdu cited both positive and negative attitudes. This comment might well sum up majority opinion as shown in other studies and DES reports: *Basically they think it's an inferior subject.*

Most pupils found the idea of a non-Asian teacher of Urdu good: they have to learn the subject from scratch, have perfect English and *it's nice to know other people are interested.* Disadvantages given were imperfect pronunciation, not being a Muslim and not being *my own kind.*

Pupils not taking Urdu

It is important to note that the parents of two-thirds of these pupils (taking German or French but not Urdu) were born outside Britain and nearly one quarter were Muslim.

Clearly these pupils had fewer reasons for choosing French/German than pupils had for choosing Urdu and showed considerably less commitment or enthusiasm. As for Urdu, very few had considered this option: *not useful, difficult, not interested* (including: *I don't like it and my parents are against it*) and *I don't think people value it as much as other languages.*

On the issue of having Urdu as an option at all, half the pupils had mixed feelings, accepting the provision but distancing themselves and especially non-Asians from it. A third made positive comments - mainly in the school where several non-Asians were learning Urdu - and some comments were very negative.

Adults' attitudes to non-Asians taking Urdu

Comments indicated that although the situation was improving *there were, and still are, quite a few people who are not happy seeing these languages introduced into schools.* Opposition was reported from pupils, teachers, parents, governors, councillors and other educationists, often on the grounds that community languages should be taught at home. Anti-Asian feelings, mere lip-service being paid to Urdu provision, and teachers of other languages feeling threatened were given as examples. No wonder that so few non-Asian pupils take Urdu.

Every teacher mentioned the difficulty of learning Urdu but with varying emphases. Other reasons given for the very slight take-up reflected the low status of Urdu outside the South-Asian community, lack of knowledge about job possibilities, and discouragement by careers officers, other teachers, parents and friends. Timetabling, the unpopularity of all languages and *I think it would take a very brave pupil - white pupil - to do it* were also cited.

Despite the above, over two-thirds of adults interviewed thought it would be better if more non-Asian pupils learnt Urdu - for multicultural and linguistic reasons. Others strongly favoured European languages - as more useful and traditional - and some feared that these would lose their popularity.

Encouraging non-Asian pupils

This question was clearly controversial - with some staff against doing so, or unsure of the advantages. Teachers felt the following to be effective: Urdu-centred assemblies and displays, popular Urdu teachers, having some non-Asian teachers of Urdu, exam passes, improved resources, and non-Asian teachers learning Urdu. Changes in school ethos and attitude of those involved in implementation of policy were also seen as important.

The possible introduction of language taster courses in the first year (e.g. several weeks each of French, German, Urdu) proved extremely contentious and most teachers and advisers expected opposition to the idea, even if they were in favour. The importance of good planning of content, materials and aims, in conjunction with teachers of other languages and bearing in mind the proposed National Curriculum, was emphasised.

Conclusions

The survey clearly showed that Urdu provision as a modern language option in the borough is popular with many pupils and teachers. Moreover, most teachers and all other educationists involved thought that the demand for Urdu classes would continue or increase over the next few years.

Many problems were described, however:

- the dearth of teachers and training possibilities and the low status of current teachers;
- the autonomy of headteachers and lack of staff support;
- the very small numbers of non-Asian pupils learning Urdu;
- the effect of the out-dated GCE syllabuses and lack of attractive materials;
- the lack of opportunities in further education.

As a result, Urdu has remained a second-rate 'ghetto' option, despite the demand for it. Some teachers and others pointed out that even if Urdu were promoted as an interesting and useful modern language option for all pupils, this would not be enough to counteract the racism within schools and society.

To end in the words of two pupils: *It's a fantastic subject and useful for us all*, but *it's got to polish up its image.*

Bengali in the mainstream school

Diana Kent

Informal and unstructured observations across the curriculum were carried out during the academic year 1986-87 with a view to identifying examples of good practice both in the teaching and the learning of Bengali and in the use of Bengali as a facilitating tool in other subject areas in a secondary girls school. The examples of practice described in this case study were located in a secondary girls' school in East London and at a mixed comprehensive in North London. I hoped to observe practice in the girls' school with the openness and naiveté of one who had not yet developed sets of attitudes pertaining to the day-to-day running of that school. My observation was divided into two parts - non-participant (just watching) and participant (acting as a support teacher).

Background

CURRICULAR ISSUES

From 1980 onwards, Bengali began to be introduced into mainstream schooling in various areas, most notably Birmingham and those parts of London where there is a high proportion of Bengali pupils.

Bengali is now becoming increasingly available as part of the core in the first year or as part of a language caroussel along with, for example, French, German and Spanish. Bengali is also included in the curriculum in some primary schools. Underpinning the curriculum at the time of the study was the rich backcloth of exposure to diverse language situations at community level: Sylheti at the spoken level and Bengali at the more formally literate level both contributed to the main stream of the Bengali language.

The acquisition of Bengali has a low currency value in society: there would appear to be very few jobs, if any, that demand a prerequisite qualification in Bengali. The Bengali teachers disputed this at an idealistic level on the basis that Bengali should be retained and encouraged for its own sake. There was pressure on the curriculum to reconcile these two polarities while at the same time presenting an educational alternative to European languages. The result was often confused.

Whether or not to adopt a cognitive or cultural approach in a syllabus, and the implications for developments in GCSE for Asian languages, also generated strong feelings. There was little evidence of internal school syllabuses.

TEACHER ISSUES

The teachers of Bengali were invariably native speakers, whereas the teachers using Bengali as a tool in other subjects were generally non-Bengali staff, sometimes working with a native speaker as support or as a team teacher.

Some staff who did not have Bengali as mother tongue took a week's intensive course, clearly motivated by the possibilities of rich pupil-pupil and teacher-pupil bilingual interaction. The teachers empathised with the difficulties that mother tongue Bengali pupils must face: their own tiredness after learning Bengali for a week gave a new dimension to how the Bengali pupils must feel dealing with English on a daily basis, and what a relief it must be for them to use the mother tongue in an environment where it is encouraged and developed.

There were very few resources for the teacher of Bengali - a fact perhaps related to unresolved curricula issues, and the staff had to spend an uncommon amount of time and energy making their own. Often, the Bengali teacher works in more than one school, and these factors combine to produce a source of passionate idealism being confounded by isolation, frustration and apparent lack of recognition. A curious paradox arises here: the more Bengali teachers work under difficult conditions, making resources, being without a syllabus, the more they are accused of being 'over-involved' or 'too emotional' and therefore not objective enough to earn enhanced status for the subject in curriculum terms or a higher salary for themselves.

PUPIL ISSUES

At a young age, i.e. eleven years, parental expectation plus a need to interact with a peer group makes Bengali readily acceptable in all forms by the Bengali pupils. Later, the brighter pupils diversify into the accepted areas of 'modern' languages as pre-requisites for further education, and there is a tendency for the Bengali options to be filled by a higher proportion of less-able pupils. It is only in the sixth form or even later that pupils return, expressing a wish for a paper qualification in Bengali. They report that 'society' expects them to have a knowledge of their own mother tongue. It is then that they realise the importance of the maintenance of Bengali both in the cultural context and as a contribution to their self esteem.

Criteria for good practice

A number of interesting models aimed at raising standards in education arise out of these general observations of the use of Bengali in schools. The models take the form of observed good practice. The criteria for good practice can be listed as follows:

1.   Evidence of achievement (Hargreaves, 1984)

      a) The passing of exams;
      b) the acquisition and application of aural and written language;
      c) whole group and small group participation and enjoyment plus the ability to work alone.

2.   Effective cross-curricular use of the language; this implies curriculum-supporting structures.

3.   Effective production and use of a variety of resources including teaching strategies and syllabuses.

4.   The capacity to generate questions and ideas.

EXAMPLES

1.   Bengali as a direct form of instruction and learning

The language teaching observed whilst working alongside a Bengali teacher favoured an informal, topic-based style leading to lively communication between teachers and learners, as in the following examples:

The class was a third-year group (twenty-one pupils) in their first year of taught Bengali, and consisted of one hundred per cent Bengali pupils. The atmosphere in the class was relaxed and friendly, and the pupils were enthusiastic in their learning. They worked readily as a class and in groups and displayed a high level of organisation and consideration for others during topic work. The subject was chosen/allocated against French and Spanish and it was hoped that some girls would take Bengali as a GCSE option. The class was taught entirely in Bengali, while the girls responded in Sylheti; this did not cause any communication problems. There was occasional English between pupils (*brilliant* and *pass me the rubber*) and between teacher and pupil (*You didn't finish yours, social environment*). (The teacher was able to communicate her intentions to the less able pupils more quickly via the use of English.) All written and reading work was in Bengali, with a wide range of starting points among the pupils: some pupils had no knowledge of the written language while others were reasonably fluent. All the pupils enjoyed reading and having stories read to them (the teacher had constructed her own readers). The work was topic-based; topics included the neighbourhood (map work, the local environment); survival needs (food, transport, clothing); and aspects of family life. Resources included worksheets, Bengali story books and a language work book, four cameras, a tape recorder, video, and presentation materials (glue, paper, scissors, etc). All work was recorded and kept in folders. It was regularly marked and the final presentation of written work in book form was of a very high standard, bound and graphically organised.

Writing presented the biggest problem for all but the most proficient pupils in Bengali, but competent writers readily helped the less proficient, using worksheets prepared by the teachers on such topics as time, number, shape, recreation, family life, clothes, with illustrations drawn from Western and Bengali cultural sources. The written work was carefully corrected and re-written and there was a strong emphasis on presentation.

2.   *Bengali as cross-curricular medium*

In my role as a participant observer I became a team teacher for six to eight weeks adding my own specialist areas of art, textile and psychology to the language resource of the Bengali teacher. The aim was to employ teaching techniques that required two teachers, as well as to produce work that could be seen and admired by the rest of the school. We devised two topics, one on jobs and services, the other on family situations. Role play and cameras were used in both topics, with the success of the first leading to a fervent desire to repeat and polish the activity a second time round. The work involved discussing different jobs and services and combining into groups to act them out before the rest of the class. Discussion ranged easily between English (for my sake) and Bengali/Sylheti between themselves and the Bengali teacher. The work involved contributions from home (magazines, props) and the pupils responded with eagerness. I took photographs which were then displayed as a sequential story with speech balloons. In the second topic the technique was refined and the pupils took their own photographs. The work was displayed in the hall and was much admired by the school.

3.   *Bengali as a tool for work in other areas*

Example 1: *The Island*[1] project in a first year English class. This project was an outstanding example of the use of Bengali as a tool, as well as the use of group work as an aid to learning and the development of self esteem. The teacher had done a good deal of research and had written up a detailed account of her work as the result of attending a course at a local English centre. She shared my own belief that group work is a good environment for language development. In her paper she detailed group-centred tasks which aimed to encourage responsibility, foster adaptability and develop social skills. Within a framework of group organisation, assessment and starting strategies, she commented on each lesson of the *Island* project under the headings of materials, activities, aims and outcome. The materials were attractively presented in English and Bengali and the emphasis was on negotiation, talk, and freedom to control activities while maintaining a sense of direction. The aims were skills-based: note-taking, drafting, negotiating (talking and listening), self-assessment; the teacher's overall assessment of the achievement of the group was most encouraging.

Curriculum structures need to be more finely tuned in schools to allow for the recognition and dissemination of such examples both within and between schools.

1.   *The Island* is based on material produced at Spencer Park school and the ILEA English Centre. ILEA English Centre, 1985.

Example 2: Quilt-making project in mathematics. The aim of this project was to encourage a more fluid social mix in the class by heightening group awareness and at the same time to stretch the mathematical abilities of the group and generalise their work into another discipline. In general, in mixed classes of Bengali and non-Bengali pupils, groups had seemed to form on the basis of race, and the groups tended not to interact. While there was no sense of conflict or tension, avoidance was paradoxically legitimised by the very success of the work in progress and there seemed to be no time for cross-cultural interaction. Certainly, the group achieved a new level of social mix based as much on the novel combination of subjects as on the re-allocation of language use. The Bengali language was being used as a tool in so far as the polarising effect of its use in the classroom was producing new and creative strategies for overcoming possible divisiveness. Each person was to design a unit for a patchwork quilt based on breaking a square down into no more than six triangles. These triangles became templates for colours of fabrics chosen, cut, and assembled in the lesson.

This project satisfied the criteria for good practice in that new strategies and ideas were generated from an existing situation.

4.   *Bengali as facilitator for learning (example contributed by Laurie Kershook).*

This example serves to show that the strategies described in the contribution do not absolutely require the presence of a Bengali-speaking teacher in the classroom for sucessful interaction to take place.

Within the context of a language awareness lesson on Greek and Greek food, a discussion arose on take-away foods in different countries. Four recently-arrived eleven-year-old Bangladeshi children with very little English as yet, identified words on a Bengali menu. They then recorded a take-away conversation in Bengali and, on their own initiative, a song in Hindi (from the Hindi videos they watched) and, finally, an excerpt from the Quran. All of these they attempted to explain in English; the urge to communicate something from their background in which others had shown interest provided a strong motivation towards acquisition of English, particularly as they realised that the language skills they already had were being valued. We may conclude that such children get a lot out of a classroom whose *lingua franca* is English, even if no specialist support is present:

- If there is more than one pupil, they use mother tongue to help make sense of the experience;
- pupils need to be allowed to talk, and not to feel that breaking silence is breaking a rule;
- a linguistic encounter is not valuable only if closely observed by the teacher. Having established the right kind of activity in the right kind of trusting context, many worthwhile learning events will occur, which the teacher may not closely observe.

There is no logic in assuming that because we cannot hear or do not understand what pupils are saying, they are deriving no educational benefit from saying it.

Conclusion

Drawing on all the examples discussed above, a number of criteria for good practice are highlighted:

- good practice is inextricably linked to good teaching; a good teacher will successfully gain and maintain the confidence of her pupils, but needs curriculum input/recognition;

- the advantages of team teaching were demonstrated: two areas of expertise in the curriculum were combined; the weekly commitment allowed time for continuity of discussion and exchange of ideas; a second teacher in the room allowed far greater objectivity from both teachers; more and better work was expected from and achieved by pupils;

- topic-based work was a useful preparation for GCSE, although the syllabus is heavily weighted with westernised topics: only three out of the twenty-one topics had a distinctly Bengali flavour and western concepts underpinned much of the teaching. It seems important to question whether the over-use of these western concepts might invalidate the essence of the language;

- the project approach allowed new strategies and ideas to be generated from an existing situation (as in the quilt-making project).

Teachers who acquired some knowledge of the Bengali language were able to develop an understanding of, and empathy with, the difficulties of pupils having to perform in a language not their own, and thus to enhance their own subject and professional areas.

IMPLEMENTING AND DEVELOPING A COHERENT POLICY

Towards effective language practice

Laurie Kershook

For the predominantly monolingual, as well as the multilingual school, similar statements of belief are applicable: that language is an essential aspect of all areas of the curriculum; that this fact must be carefully considered and its implications explored; that no pupils must be led to believe that any aspects of the culture or language brought from home are insignificant or inferior; that pupils should not be expected to leave at the school gates essential components of their personalities and experience in terms of the language and culture of their homes.

It is useful, nevertheless, to examine the kind of language policy criteria which might be relevant to the needs of the multilingual school, and to compare them with some criteria for the school which is predominantly monolingual.

Making the policy work

This book takes it as axiomatic that every school, whether predominantly monolingual or multilingual, needs to have a language policy.

The notion of a language policy is given some support by the Kingman Committee (Kingman, 1988)[1], but in this context there is a great deal of confusion between the terms 'language' and 'languages'. These confusions are practical as well as conceptual; let us look at the conceptual problems first.

There is a need for language policy makers to make clear distinctions between their concepts. Are we, for example, to claim to pupils that all languages, dialects and accents are equally prestigious, when we know that in reality they are not?

In stressing the value of linguistic diversity, either in terms of language other than English or varieties of English itself, are we valuing pupils' cultures and thus contributing to their well-being, but at the same time depriving them of what we know to be the language of access to influence and power?

How are we to ensure that our policy is truly about language, even though to a great extent it is concerned with the role of languages?

1. p48, ch.4, para 50-52.

Having attempted to distinguish between these two concepts, how do we go about agreeing on what kinds of approach to language should pervade the whole curriculum?

In British culture, language has traditionally been an agent for division and conflict rather than a tool for unity. The Kingman report, with its insistence on the value of 'Standard English' does little to counteract this divisiveness. The question of language is a battlefield on which two major issues are currently being fought. First, there is the campaign to establish the skilful use of Standard English as a marker against which all kinds of language proficiency are to be measured; hence the Kingman report as a herald of the National Curriculum. That issue creates the second: the struggle to retain the concept of 'belonging'. The view is often expressed that support of mother tongues and heritage cultures is harmful to ethnic minority communities as it encourages 'ghettoisation'. Some even believe that living in Britain implies an obligation to assimilate English culture and speak the English language. The kind of language one speaks, or is able to speak, or wishes to speak, must not come to be taken as indicative of one's right to belong within defined contexts in our society, or even to belong in it at all.

Some teachers, governors or members of the community in inner city schools may object to the high priority placed on bilingualism in a language policy and instead attach overriding importance to improving immigrant pupils' English as the key to success in examinations and, therefore, in the wider society.

A major source of conflict is the lack of agreement as to what strategies are really in the best interests of the pupils. It follows that an essential element in the creation of a language policy is the assessment of the particular needs of the pupils for whom the policy is intended.

Given the range and intensity of views, it cannot be stressed sufficiently how necessary it is, in forming a language policy, to proceed according to the best guidelines of curriculum development: define objectives and tasks; delegate responsibility; invite wide participation; consult frequently and invite criticism; be prepared to modify or change; allow a realistic time scale; allocate sufficient resources; disseminate frequent progress reports; evaluate at regular intervals.

By being aware of the pitfalls and proceeding with an understanding of the daunting complexity of the task, the establishing of a worthwhile and effective language policy which satisfies all kinds of needs is more likely to be achieved.

Deciding on a policy

A secondary school's structure does not lend itself easily to the establishment of an effective network of strategies for creating and implementing a language policy; it is virtually impossible to arrive at one policy which will be to the satisfaction of all those concerned in formulating it. It is, however, essential for schools to have a language policy which has been arrived at by means of an extensive process of involvement; the whole-curriculum value of the exercise can be recognised by involving representatives from all areas of the curriculum in the consultation process, so that the strategies, when implemented, will be seen to be consistent with a practical and realistic blueprint, sanctioned by all. The policy will thus carry weight and will exert influence on the whole curriculum, in accordance with the recommendation of the Bullock report (Bullock, 1975), encouraging colleagues to go forward with confidence. The policy needs to state clearly the school's expectations of its teachers and pupils. It needs to state clear aims and the means by which, as well as the time-scale within which, it intends to achieve them.

A coordinating group, meeting regularly, representing various curriculum aspects, and including teachers who have particularly relevant skills, experience or responsibilities, can provide an effective forum for wide participation. The timetabling, for instance, of mother tongue support and community language teaching presents many logistical problems, as it involves catering for part-classes and part-teachers, sometimes in conjunction with the timetables of other schools who share the services of support teams or peripatetic teachers. A reluctant timetabler can severely retard the implementation of a sound language policy. A willing, co-operative and creative timetabler, however, can provide the enabling drive which turns blueprint into reality.

Central to the tasks are those whose work is directly concerned with language and languages: teachers of mother tongues, foreign modern languages, English language and English as a Second Language, and teachers in 'learning support' departments; but community representatives, school governors and LEA advisers should also be invited to make contributions.

Such a group should be given its mandate by the headteacher, and ideally should be working within the framework of existing published LEA policies on education, language, racial equality and equality of opportunity. These are likely to embody criteria which apply to all schools in terms of the creation and implementation of the policy:

- the whole staff must establish ownership of the policy by working on and developing it over a considerable period of time;

- it must reflect the realities of society in general, but must also reflect the needs of the individual school;

- the policy's criteria must be clear, practical and achievable, and should influence all curriculum areas;

- the implementation process must be linked to a carefully planned and budgeted programme of whole-staff, departmental and individual in-service training;

- progress needs to be recorded, monitored, and evaluated. When necessary, practice should be modified in the light of experience.

Some strategies for implementation

The following check list of good language practice, although not exhaustive, may conveniently be grouped under three areas of consideration:

Pastoral and cross-curricular strategies

In a multilingual school which has an effective language policy:

● Details of the ethnolinguistic background of pupils are known, in terms of which languages other than English are spoken in the home; which of these languages are spoken by the pupil and how well; which pupils attend community supplementary schools, whether with a primarily linguistic or religious brief. Those with specific pastoral responsibilities are aware of the importance of the mother tongues spoken by pupils, and display a positive attitude to them. Pupils' mother tongues are taken into account when considering placement in tutor groups.

● Naming systems which differ from the European convention are understood.

● Details of languages spoken by pupils and parents are requested on admission to the school and recorded. Letters home are multilingual, as are signs and notices around the school, and displays of pupils' work.

● Assemblies are multilingual; bilingual members of staff or visitors from outside are invited to them and parts of them are conducted in the pupils' mother tongues.

● Teachers learn some basics of the mother tongues mainly represented.

● Classes or groups consisting mainly or entirely of non-English speakers are not allowed to be formed. Such pupils are provided with suitable and useful learning tasks, through which they have reasonable chance of experiencing success.

● The school library and form-room libraries contain good selections of bilingual books and books in community languages suitable for a wide range of ages and abilities. Pupils are encouraged to use their mother tongues/community languages in the classroom, especially for the purposes of collaborative learning where their use may aid the processes of creative or deductive thought.

● Those who speak any language other than English are given the opportunity to extend that knowledge, or to use their skill in a non-standard variety as a basis of their study of a standard form.

● Those whose knowledge of the mother tongue is vestigial, or characterised by diglossia, are encouraged to revive and extend their skills.

● The ESL department co-ordinates strategies of language learning by means of in-class support. The subject matter of any withdrawal lessons is based on mainstream curriculum content, and not on theoretical language work.

● Pupils who are beginners in the English language are given access to the curriculum via the use of their mother tongue, in the form of in-class support from bilingual teachers and the use of bilingual books and worksheets.

Languages departments

In languages departments in schools:

● The term 'modern language' is not used in contrast to 'community language'.

● The main languages of the community are offered from year 1 in addition to or as alternatives to the traditional French, German or Spanish, and pupils with no family connection with these languages are encouraged to opt for them.

● Teachers of these languages have the skills to cater for the differing needs of a wide range of community language learners.

● All pupils are given 'taster' lessons in the principal community languages, as part of an introductory course to language study.

● A 'Language Awareness' course is taught at some point, usually during the first year, outlining the history of the English language, providing an introduction to the mechanics of languages and the process of language learning, and showing how the English language and culture have grown from a multiplicity of influences in a continuing process. It also shows the ways in which many languages are in everyday use in Britain, including in the school itself.

● The largest portion of the body of knowledge and experience to be transmitted stems from the pupils themselves. The role of the teacher is to listen and learn along with them and stimulate discussion and thought.

● There is close co-operation with local Community Supplementary Schools, especially those which share the school's premises. Reciprocal visits take place, and help with resources is provided. There are opportunities for exchange of expertise. Pupils are made aware of the links, and encouraged to attend the supplementary schools.

The monolingual school

Every education authority and every school needs a language policy; this need is by no means restricted to schools which have significant or large numbers of ethnic minority pupils. In accepting the general principles set forward above for a language policy for multilingual and monolingual schools, a monolingual school may well discover that its pupil population is nowhere near as monolingual as it had seemed. The school may wish to examine its pupils' use of accents, dialects and slang in English - practices not entirely dissimilar from the use of mother tongues - for the purpose of extending the repertoire of speech registers, so as not to represent language, culture and knowledge as static, rigid, classless concepts, for which change, in the shape of new influences, means corruption. There is value in careful analyses of the processes of trial and error through which learners acquire the relevant linguistic repertoires in particular languages for particular contexts and for particular purposes. The next stage of development of a language policy in the predominantly monocultural school might then be the introduction of new topics into the curriculum.

One section of a 'Language Awareness' course might be to trace the diverse influences on the language, literature and culture of England over many centuries, thereby prompting a re-examination of notions of 'purity' and emphasising the effects of migration and interculturalism on language and culture. Causes and effects of migration should also feature in social and political education, history, sociology and economics.

Conclusion

Schools which claim that their contribution to multicultural education is to 'treat everyone the same' are missing the essential and fundamental point: everyone is not the same, and our education system must show that we understand and value that fact and do not attribute to any single ethnic group, culture, class, accent, language or religion more 'right to belong' than we attribute to any other.

Resources and materials for teaching a wider range of languages

John Broadbent

This article is based on a Working Paper prepared for the EC Pilot Project: Community Languages in the Secondary Curriculum *by the Coordinator, John Broadbent. It draws heavily on the Project's Final Report, and on written suggestions volunteered by Pratap Deshpande, Elena Mardegan and Kuldip Singh Rai.*

The range of languages offered in British secondary schools is extremely narrow. Indeed, without the recent attempts to include some of the languages used by pupils in their homes and local communities, the range would probably be declining rather than growing. One of the most commonly mentioned impediments to a desirable diversification in the language curriculum has been the lack of relevant materials which can be used in particular to support the current emphasis on developing the communicative competences of the learners. Publishing houses suggest that it is only for French that the market is sufficiently large to justify adequate ongoing investment in new coursebooks for schools. With respect to the languages already known to groups of pupils within a particular school population, however, there are rich resources waiting to be tapped in terms of existing skills amongst teachers for whom these languages are the mother tongue. There are living resources circulating in each of the linguistic communities whose children attend neighbourhood schools, especially in inner cities. And there are resources already in the heads of many of the pupils who have chosen to extend their knowledge of a community language as a part of their secondary education. The creation of the kinds of coursebook used for French is less relevant for this area of language teaching: packages based on particular themes which can be exploited at different levels and in different teaching contexts may well provide a more relevant resource. More flexible publishing systems can now be called upon to assist: these operate either from photocopyable matrices, or microcomputers and national database networks.

The Pilot Project funded by the European Commission from 1984 to 1987, entitled *Community Languages in the Secondary Curriculum* explored the available resources with respect to Italian, Panjabi and Urdu. In general terms, it criticised the use of materials which had been imported from countries in which these languages were a main medium of schooling. Such materials rarely, if ever, combined content relevant to the maturity of secondary school pupils in England with a level of language which was not utterly intimidating. To this extent, the findings of HMI (1984) and Molteno (1986) were confirmed. Materials which had been prepared with a view to teaching the three languages as foreign languages were, moreover, seen to be inadequate, since they failed to take into account the possibility that each language might well be used in the immediate locality of the teaching environment; the existing linguistic knowledge of the learners had tended therefore to be ignored, or regarded as an impediment in the acquisition of standard forms.

This existing knowledge - as is demonstrated by the case studies in this volume - might vary in a single classroom from complete fluency and literacy to slight passive knowledge of a closely related language or dialect. Despite the potential for exploiting locally-used languages as the raw material for helping pupils to extend their linguistic repertoires, it emerged that few of the strategies employed really suited the educational purposes intended, and that virtually no coherent programme of teaching existed which could take full account of the existing knowledge of the learners.

The EC Pilot Project evolved a procedure for the creation, circulation and eventual dissemination of good practice, which is being taken forward by Birmingham, Inner London and Nottinghamshire, the local education authorities which took part in the Project. In a separate development, *Multilingk*, the Inter-Authority Committee for Community Language materials, has been formed to develop a bank of material for community languages, including requirements for GCSE examinations in the first instance, and, in the longer term, to work on examination syllabuses and assessment techniques. The system operates through the pooled efforts of LEAs active in provision of the teaching of community languages, and information on progress will be disseminated through the Centre for Information on Language Teaching and Research. Other strands, particularly the debate on methodology, are continuing under the auspices of the Multilingual Initiative, based with the Centre for Multicultural Education at the University of London Institute of Education. The preparation of teaching materials for community languages in secondary schools continues, unfortunately, to be seen largely as the preparation of worksheets, and the value of using a variety of media is often neglected.

Improved materials have been created often as a result of the intervention of the European Commission, especially for Greek, Italian and Turkish, but non-European languages have been largely neglected. There are still insufficient funds and time allocated to practising teachers to realise their ideas in terms of professionally produced resources. All too often, the development of teaching materials has been based on goodwill and spare time commitment. More satisfactory results depend on the construction of new projects to which bilingual teachers can be fully seconded to engage in development work.

Catalogues of existing materials

Despite the general inadequacy of most existing resources, it is nevertheless useful to maintain a list of the ones which are proving to be of use, however limited. It is useful also to collect reviews by practising teachers, detailing the features of such resources. Successful formats for this enterprise have been developed for Italian (Baldwin, 1983) and for Bengali (ILEA, 1987). At the outset of the EC Pilot Project, catalogues and consumer reports were compiled of the published materials being used by the participants. Some of these reports were eventually published in the relevant professional journals, most notably the *Journal of the Association of Teachers of Italian.*
The usefulness of existing materials, and the development of improved resources can be considered from five main points of view:

1 the salient features of the contexts in which individual community languages are taught and used;
2 the categories of learners developing their knowledge of these languages and their differing needs;
3 the particularities of each specific language;
4 the kinds of experience and information which should be made available through the provision in schools of community languages;
5 the standards to be set in the production of purpose-made teaching materials.

The five points of view can be summed up in five key words, - 'context', 'learners', 'language', 'content' and 'quality'. Each of these is the focus for separate analyses below. The section on 'content' has been extended to include a framework for storing and retrieving materials, whilst the section on 'quality' includes guidelines for the circulation and trialling of innovatory approaches.

Context

When we talk about the teaching of any particular language as a community language, we are essentially talking about the context in which the learning takes place. Strictly speaking, in many educational contexts in the United Kingdom, Chinese, Italian, Urdu and many other languages are not simply 'modern foreign languages', the term used in National Curriculum documentation leading up to the Education Reform Act (1988). The fact is that they are also indigenous languages in the UK and are used in sizable speech communities here. Just as the term 'Teaching English as a Second Language' was used to clarify the insight that for learners in Britain a foreign language methodology was not appropriate, so too now for 'Teaching Chinese or Italian or Urdu as a Community Language'; we can say that the methodology will need to relate at least in part to the circumstances under which the language is used in the United Kingdom. Prevailing attitudes to different languages can vary according to a whole range of factors, some of which are suggested in the case studies section of this volume. The preparation of relevant materials would consequently need to take account of such factors. For example, the prestige which a particular language commands locally will be a factor which not only determines the numbers of pupils choosing that language in an option scheme, it will also have a direct bearing on the range of situations in which the language is commonly used, and on the purposes to which the students may be encouraged to extend their knowledge. In the classroom the teaching process may be deployed towards a variety of objectives, such as:

- to foster the capacity to communicate and to think in the language;
- to transmit elements of the culture in which the language evolved;
- to increase ability to analyse features of society that impinge upon the learners, and to help them to articulate

117

and deal with the issues that concern members of that community in this society;

- to develop particular attitudes and skills, including the exploration of concepts and skills required in other parts of the curriculum;
- to assist in the analysis and understanding of structures in the particular languages, as well as in others.

In order to extend even further beyond the range of private uses to which mother tongue speakers currently deploy their knowledge in the UK, materials will need also to relate to a perhaps more restricted range of public settings in which *ab initio* learners of the specific community languages might also come to use the new knowledge they acquire. The first such setting is the classroom itself with its own peculiar forms of discourse. Other relevant settings in which the conveying and understanding of messages is made easier by contextual support may be simulated in the classroom, or may draw upon interaction which can be encouraged beyond the classroom. In the context of the classroom itself, the maximum possible use should be made of the language for exchanges between teacher and student; early familiarisation with the functions of language needed for successful classroom interaction is desirable.

This is of course now widely recommended with reference to foreign language learning contexts as well, the common aim being to come closer to a natural language learning situation. The crucial difference between the framework proposed here and that which is currently being suggested for foreign language syllabuses lies in its definition of the principal role of the learner as 'oppressed resident' rather than as 'tourist' or interpreter. Settings and topics need to be selected with a clearer relevance to the actual contexts in which community languages are used in specific localities in Britain. Drawing on the insights of students and teachers of each language, lists of relevant settings can easily be compiled and might usefully include educational institutions; the homes of community language speakers; locations in predominantly urban environments in which speakers of the various languages assemble, such as places of entertainment, parks, sports centres, places of worship, eating places, shops, community centres, health centres, political gatherings, workplaces and so on; agencies with which they have to deal, such as rates offices, travel agents, hospitals, Department of Health and Social Security, Home Office. Within each of the specific settings identified, it is of value to list the related tasks which students might wish to be able to perform.

When languages are taught as community languages in schools where a high proportion of the population uses them, the presence of native speakers enhances the learning environment considerably, especially for any beginners who happen to be present. The process benefits from the existence of realia and authentic materials which circulate within the linguistic communities themselves - invitation cards, food labels, books, newspapers, tape-recordings of poems and songs, videos and films. It becomes possible to envisage authentic communicative uses of language which, although greatly desired, are simply not possible in most modern language classrooms as they exist today.

On the other hand, negative attitudes to the use for educational purposes of any language other than English (or possibly French and German) are so deep-seated that even where the possibilities of actually using the target language are high, inhibiting psychological factors inevitably come into play. A sympathetic understanding of each individual learner is crucial.

LEARNERS

Most teachers of community languages have as their students young people who have taken a conscious and deliberate decision to develop their knowledge of the language or languages of their parental heritage. Many such young people have, however, begun to lose touch with their heritage, and are in need of encouragement to make it their own again. In order to be of assistance to them in this endeavour, it is necessary to predict, more clearly than they can, the purposes to which their knowledge can be put, and the difficulties that will be encountered in the process of learning.

Careful recording and analysis of case studies is necessary to bring teachers closer to an understanding of the ways in which their students use and acquire language. Students who have already mastered a language in addition to their mother tongue can call on strategies beyond imitation and unconscious experimentation; they can consciously compare and contrast different languages, and strengthen their knowledge of one language via another. Preferred learning strategies mentioned by students involved in the Project included various strategies and techniques which in the main have been discarded by the language teaching profession: copying, translation and learning by heart were often used to supplement the more generally accepted discovery processes generated by immersion in a context in which the language is used for real communication, or by the teacher drawing attention to the internal logic of grammatical structures. Whole class activities need to be complemented by group assignments and individually programmed activities geared to preferred learning styles in such a way as to foster increasing independence in the learner.

Teaching materials which can realise the aim of developing learner independence will, as far as possible, be self-explanatory both for teacher and students. Instructions about how to use the material will need to be clear and easy to follow. Much of the work of trialling and implementation benefits greatly from the presence of more than one teacher in the classroom, especially when poorly motivated and disruptive pupils may be present.

Analysis of the kinds of competence identified amongst learners of community languages suggests different levels of teaching target to be located somewhere between specialised skills for fluent users of the community language (such as story-telling, translation, public speaking, and so on) and a transactional foundation for students who may have no knowledge of the language, and no family connections with it. Effective teaching materials should consequently address the different levels of existing competence by devising tasks at different levels of difficulty around a repeating series of themes, such that overall cohesion can be maintained in a classroom containing a wide range of individual attainment.

Many teachers have encouraged students to take part in the design of materials of closer relevance to learners of their own language in Britain. It becomes an integral part of the teaching strategy to draw on the creative talents of the pupils themselves. One concrete result of such a strategy has been a board game produced at Clapham College in the ILEA; the game is based on the small businesses run by Italian families in the neighbourhood of the school. Elsewhere this kind of approach has resulted in students making up their own cartoon illustrations and texts, often in the form of dialogues, which can then be used as materials by other learners. This procedure is difficult and perhaps raises as many questions as it solves, but it can undoubtedly contribute to the coherence with which students approach their learning.

Descriptions of more sophisticated personal uses of language can be elicited from students who already have extensive knowledge of the language being taught, or of a closely related one; the more reflective uses to which they may put their language often prove to be relatively context-free, whereas transactional tasks are almost always context embedded. Reflective tasks have included private uses of language such as intimate conversations; reading for information and pleasure; and writing personal accounts in the form of letters or a diary. Lists of themes for discussions and project work can thus be compiled and negotiated with particular classes. From such lists can be extrapolated details of the themes of age, gender, and linguistic background.

It was noted that many of the themes suggested as being relevant for teaching of Italian, Panjabi and Urdu also offer scope for practising the functions of language required for dealing with them in the settings listed in a Transactional Foundation. For the student already possessing a high level of fluency and literacy, the presentation of the same themes could be pitched at even higher levels of sophistication in order to form the subject of speeches and debates; practice in advanced skills of interpreting and translation could easily be offered in the kind of simulated settings recommended above, whilst literary texts, exercises in creative writing and other assignments related to professional uses of language, such as interview techniques, or related to social and cultural uses of language, such as story telling or poetry recital, could be chosen for their relevance to themes and settings as previously specified.

LANGUAGE

Teachers share with applied linguists an enormous problem of describing to their own and to their students' satisfaction the ways in which living languages function, and can be acquired. Current research into the stages of development towards mastery of any language suggests that many of the processes of early naturalistic acquisition are also followed by learners at a higher stage of maturity. The stages of development may vary from language to language, but general principles can nevertheless be discerned. The acquisition of individual languages systems seems often to follow a predictable sequence to which any teaching programme for that particular language must relate, and there is potentially great value in careful analyses of the processes of trial and error through which learners extend their linguistic repertoire in particular contexts, in particular languages, and for particular purposes. Purposeful learning syllabuses will either be constructed out of an ongoing analysis of needs, or will arise from a threshold-type enumeration of those notions and functions which are intuitively believed to be of general application, but which can be confirmed through negotiation with the students themselves. Our knowledge is insufficiently detailed to identify what might prove to be the easiest starting points, what errors might be regarded as acceptable at different stages of language acquisition, or, indeed, what developments might constitute progress in the acquisition and use of particular languages. In whichever way the syllabuses are arrived at, it has to be recognised that the linguistic content of a community language course will be quite different from the static grammatical/lexical teaching lists already developed for many foreign languages. It must also be recognised, however, that in the secondary phase we are promoting varieties and registers of language which, although based on the languages used in the community and in the homes of many of the pupils, may lie beyond the current experience of learners in schools.

In the EC Pilot Project, the exponents of language to be consciously transmitted for use for educational and social purposes were selected according to the following criteria:

-    frequency and naturalness of use by mother tongue speakers;

-    conformity with educational standards in the original language areas;

-    relevance and utility within the context of a multilingual but often racist society;

-    feasibility, taking into account structural complexities as well as the experience and capabilities of learners.

There is often a tension between these different criteria, especially the first two. The concepts of 'repertoire', 'register' and 'appropriacy' are helpful in resolving some of these tensions. All users of a particular language possess a wide repertoire of different forms between which it is possible to switch, depending on the person addressed and the context. Viewed in this way, 'appropriate' language varies according to setting and relationship; it depends upon the broad social relationships between users, or upon the subject matter under discussion; the differences are often referred to as differences of 'style' or 'register'.

In educational contexts beyond the primary phase it would seem appropriate to be promoting the language accepted by educated speakers and writers, indeed to be pointing our students in the direction of the most creative but also the most simple and lucid uses of language which can be encountered in modern texts. We have nevertheless to take maximum advantage of the existing language knowledge of our students and to guard against adopting a deprecating attitude to the ways in which they find it comfortable to express themselves. In the development of community languages as fully valid parts of the mainstream secondary school curriculum, with all that that entails in terms of formal argument and exposition, academic discourse, and literary appreciation, we need also to take careful stock of the enriching possibilities which exist within our society for the communicative use of the locally available languages.

CONTENT

It has been stated above that teaching materials for languages taught as community languages need to relate to the experience, enthusiasms and existing language repertoires of our students if a positive transfer of knowledge is to be effected. We would, however, be failing in our endeavour to educate, if our materials did not take the students beyond the forms of knowledge and experience which are already available to them. The informational content of the texts we place before students will require careful consideration not merely from the standpoint of familiarity, but also with regard to its relation to other subjects in the curriculum, and to its ability to foster a confident sense of identification with the culture associated with the language learned. In practice this means that although initial teaching materials should be based on the experience of children born and brought up in the United Kingdom, the offering of alternative perceptions, particularly those which are rooted in the forms of culture associated with each individual language, should be progressively encouraged.

Content should be taken to include not only subject matter, but also learning and teaching processes. Experiential learning involves a concern for the issues and activities which students can focus on whilst extending their linguistic knowledge. It demands answers as to what school-based projects, and what linguistic products could find an interested audience in the classroom, in the rest of the school (or other schools), and in the local neighbourhood. Different groups of students learning Italian in South Wales have created audiences for themselves by translating a tourist brochure, and by supplying a children's page for the local magazine which circulates amongst the Italian community. Arising from the circulation of the first draft of a guide to letter-writing in Italian, the whole team of teachers based with the *Ufficio Scolastico (Londra 2)* has begun collecting examples of authentic letters as sent and received by their pupils.

An important component of this strategy for providing students with an audience for their skills involves older pupils talking over the most favoured kinds of stories with younger ones. Vocational courses in a number of Birmingham schools encourage students to go and recount stories in various languages in the feeder primary schools. Other forms of active learning include catering for visitors to the school, conducting surveys of local shopping facilities, campaigning against a deportation, taping reminiscences of older members of their communities, adapting and playing games, designing teaching materials for use with younger or less proficient classes. Role-play, simulation, poetry and songs, shared writing, silent reading, discussions, class visits, project work, practical work, local environmental research, mime and drama have all been used more or less successfully.

It is self-evident that no teaching materials can be culturally neutral. Culturally loaded images are present in the earliest primers onwards, including those used for example for developing early literacy in Urdu. The culture displayed in these primers may be in some ways unfamiliar to learners, who may have been born and brought up in Britain. Pictures of houses, streets and policemen are as unfamiliar as the descriptions of weather conditions. A sensible compromise would involve portraying the existing norms for both societies, but there remains of course the question as to which section of the society any cultural norm can be taken to reflect.

Success in developing a transferability in particular approaches from one language to another, or indeed from one context to another, is proving to be elusive. It would seem that practically all of the resources which have so far been made available are insufficiently accessible for any users other than their immediate designers.

Community language teaching materials which have shown themselves to be of value to broad constituencies of learners of specific languages, such as Mubashar (1987) and Khan (1982), are planned around thematic learning centres, each one with elements which can be approached in different ways for different year groups, depending on their relative levels of knowledge and maturity. This means, for example, that although the main parts of thematic learning centres which might focus on the local environment would be envisaged in the first instance for students with close family connections in the local community which uses the language, certain simple assignments related to that same learning centre might suitably be offered also to younger students with little or no contact as yet with that community.

Clearly much depends on the age and experience of the individual learners, but it is not impossible to envisage the design of components of increasing complexity within each thematic learning centre: indeed, a pattern already exists in the kinds of lesson content and teaching technique which participating teachers have so far found to be most successful. Forward planning allows for activities around a repeating series of learning centres to be offered year by year: the structure of the syllabus thus becomes cyclical, with an inbuilt process for revision and consolidation, which nevertheless caters for the students' developing maturity in terms of interests, and is sufficiently flexible to incorporate topical issues. In this way it becomes possible to relate flexibly and directly to the processes of language acquisition observed in individual students or groups of students. No existing course book could relate to the wide range of attainment encountered in classrooms where community languages are taught. Instead, it seems sensible to compile packages of materials and references which relate to particular thematic content. The learning centres proposed below may seem somewhat arbitrary but they have helped to create structure and continuity within a range of different teaching programmes in different languages:

Personal Details; Social Events; Environment; Classroom Instruction; Communication and Media.

Under each of these headings it is possible to suggest a core of graded assignments whereby students and teachers can come to recognise the progress made. Many of the assignments which have been tried at the more advanced levels of performance find an echo in other subjects taught in the school curriculum. The comparison of the features of extended and nuclear families which belongs with a unit on Personal Details, for example, is often a part of Sociology, or Social Studies. Planning a meal for guests, which is part of Social Events relates also to Home Economics, and so on.

Given the kinds of syllabus which have been developed, and the currently available levels of expertise, there would seem to be value in creating a series of resource banks which could be stored in filing cabinets or in a computerised database. Such a system would ease the retrieval of materials based around a single unified learning centre but aimed towards differentiated levels of linguistic competence, different previous experience, different interests, and so on. Recent developments in educational technology, such as, for example, the National Educational Resources Information Service (NERIS) database, mean that teaching materials for a number of community languages can be stored on computer, and printed out or amended to suit the needs of particular groups of students.

QUALITY

The quality of printed and other teaching materials for community languages needs to be at least as good as it is for other subjects in the curriculum. Unfortunately, in the urgent drive to create teaching materials, and in some cases to publish and sell them privately, teachers of community languages have in some cases acted hastily, putting materials on to the market which have not been tried in their own classrooms, and which have not been checked for gross errors. The preparation of teaching materials for community languages in secondary schools continues, unfortunately, to be seen largely as the preparation of worksheets, and the value of using a variety of media is often neglected. Although curriculum development support units in different local education authorities, and the EC Pilot Project itself, have assisted in the printing and distribution of individually produced materials, this assistance has not yet proved to offer a viable return in either pedagogical or financial terms.

All examples of teaching materials need to be produced to professional standards before circulation to other teachers, and the potential for their use needs to be immediately clear. In submitting examples of their best materials for exhibition and circulation, teachers should supply all details of the gender, social class, and ethnic composition of the school, the place of the language within the curriculum, the rationale for its introduction, the intercultural initiatives taken elsewhere in the curriculum, the support for the language in the local community in terms of parental demand and supplementary school provision, the proportions of native speakers opting to study it, and so on. Given the raw state of teaching materials so far developed for teaching community languages, these contextual factors are as necessary a preface to all examples of practice, as are the immediate aims and objectives. Equally important is the need for some indication accompanying a set of materials as to whether they have actually been tested in the classroom, and what the outcomes were of their use.

There is a healthy tendency for community language teachers to wish to create their own materials with particular groups of students in mind. Some colleagues have argued that teachers do not in fact need ready-made teaching units, but methodological guidance and some supporting examples. This is not to deny the value of marketing ready-made materials of high quality, since few teachers are likely to possess the technical skills of syllabus design, or art-work and layout which could result in a product of general use. Some centralisation e.g. *Multilingk* and AIMER, is clearly necessary in order to maintain high standards of production and to reduce the wastage of effort involved. The successful development of teaching resources cannot be based merely on goodwill or on a spare time commitment, which means for example that supply teachers must be found to replace teachers engaged in development work.

Staff at the BBC and the commissioning editors of various publishing houses are beginning to recognise that there are possibilities for the development and publication of new course materials for community languages. Few if any of the publishers or local education authorities which have in the past worked separately have the staff or the materials resources that are called for. Different sorts of collaboration and different sources of funding are necessary for adequate materials production: a national programme is needed, with posts advertised and filled by specially seconded and fully trained teachers for all of the community languages which have begun to find a relevant place in the curriculum of British schools. There is a strong case for building up a national team with proven ability in the design of materials. Finance has been made available for the promotion of Welsh in this way, but not as yet for the other languages of the United Kingdom.

Teacher training in multilingual Britain

Guy Merchant

Attempts to train teachers to meet the needs of pupils and their schools in a rapidly changing multilingual society are for the most part poorly documented. Despite successive waves of enthusiasm in in-service work, initial teacher training has been slow to respond to the challenge of linguistic diversity. Atkins (1985) in a summary of the research commissioned by the Swann Committee to investigate the training of language teachers describes the problem areas. These include student recruitment, lack of relevant staff expertise and the absence of an appropriate model. Since this work was carried out, some small-scale initiatives have been launched which illustrate ways in which problems might be addressed in a constructive manner. However, these developments are mostly ad hoc measures drawn up in the absence of coherent policy on the place of community languages in the school curriculum.

Although community language teachers are an essential resource in the development of positive approaches to linguistic diversity, it is easy to overlook the role of monolingual teachers and, for that matter, their bilingual colleagues who may have no desire to contribute directly to the language teaching enterprise. For some time there has been concern over the short supply of teachers from the ethnic minorities. CRE Report (Ranger, 1988) offers documentary evidence of this. Posts requiring specialist community language teachers are often hard to fill, but to use the lack of trained community language teachers as an excuse for not recognising the linguistic resources of community and society at large is to underestimate the creativity of both teachers and pupils. Language awareness courses in secondary schools along the line of the work of the primary school teachers recorded in *All Our Languages* (Houlton, 1985) act as a signpost, showing colleagues how all staff can contribute to work relevant to a linguistically diverse society.

Training needs

Khan (1985) in her sharp critique of the Swann Report's chapter on language education, suggests that one of its more useful contributions to the debate has been to distinguish between the language needs of all pupils - an awareness of linguistic diversity - and the specific language needs of ethnic minority pupils. As Khan observes, the report says relatively little by way of practical guidance on how the needs of all pupils can be met, and is decidedly disappointing with respect to bilingual pupils. Brumfit's 'charter of rights' offers a more stable framework for exploring the curricular implications of linguistic diversity for both multilingual and monolingual schools.

The development of a positive educational response to the languages of Britain has implications for the training of teachers. Training needs can be looked at in two ways. First, there are the basics that all teachers need as part of their professional preparation for work in a multilingual society. For example, teachers need to be informed about the linguistic diversity in Britain, and to be aware of the language needs of bilingual pupils as well as the lack of bargaining power of some linguistic minorities; but above all student teachers ought to know something about the significance of languages and varieties to particular communities and language users. Through developing an awareness of multilingualism in our society, students, like the pupils they will eventually teach, will be encouraged to adopt a favourable attitude to the various language groups. In practical terms, training institutions should seek to equip these students with a range of skills and strategies which will enable them to use linguistic diversity as a reference point in planning language activity in a variety of contexts.

Secondly, there is a need for bilingual teachers as part of the established staffing and management of schools. In this category we would include teachers with a wide variety of subject specialisms who have first hand experience of life in a bilingual community. Their needs, in terms of course provision, are no different from those mentioned above, although their interest may on occasions be more specific than some of their monolingual colleagues. Within this group there is, however, a pressing need to recruit more community language teachers - essentially such teachers are defined as those who train to teach an ethnic minority language or languages as a subject specialism. It is important to consider the supply of both bilingual teachers and specialist community language teachers. This distinction is an important one if we are to avoid falling into the trap of assuming that anyone who is bilingual will automatically wish to teach in both languages.

All teachers

It is not uncommon to hear teacher trainers, advisers and INSET providers arguing that all teachers should have a general awareness of linguistic diversity as well as some specific skills in fostering positive attitudes in their pupils to the languages and varieties of contemporary Britain. This particular form of language awareness was endorsed by the Swann Committee. In one of the more prescriptive statements concerning the role of induction courses and INSET in preparing teachers for multilingual classrooms, the Swann Report suggests that teachers should:

> ... have an increased awareness of the particular languages used by their pupils including an ability to identify which language an individual child is speaking, to identify various scripts and at the very least to be able to pronounce a child's name correctly.

(Swann Report 1985, 2.17)

Apart from this, the only central Government recommendations are to be found in the many DES statements that succinctly suggest that all teachers should be aware of the ethnic and linguistic diversity of the school population (for instance, DES Circular 3/84). How this awareness is to be developed, and translated into practical and informed decisions on learning methodology and content and the selection of resources, remains to be fully explored.

Arora's (1986) case study of change in initial teacher training shows how an institution can adapt to meet a shifting pattern of demands. Change, argues Arora, will continue:

> ... as long as an institutional structure has been created within which programmes can be adapted to the needs of an urban multiracial, multicultural and multilingual community and as long as the college acknowledges a responsibility for social action and a continuing need to provide teachers with a conceptual framework which enables them constantly to re-examine their own knowledge and skills.

Bradford and Ilkley's academic policy informs various aspects of its BEd degrees. For instance, the college's 'Language and

Literature' subject specialism incorporates the study of a South-Asian language - available to both monolingual and bilingual students. Progress in oracy and literacy is assessed on a sliding scale which takes into account differences in initial competence. Students wishing to develop language-related classroom skills can follow a 'Language in Education' elective which introduces current theory and research in first and second language acquisition.

A small-scale review of BEd degree courses conducted by the LDIP project (Merchant, 1987) shows how different training institutions have developed responses to linguistic diversity. The variety in interpretations documented is often related to the background and expertise of academic staff and it is with this in mind that the LDIP project is now developing ways of meeting the needs of initial teacher trainers. At a seminar[1] organised by the project, teacher trainers began to identify the important ingredients of training for linguistic diversity. These are summarised in Table 1 (on page 133).

Clearly initial training has a long way to go in evolving ways of representing linguistic diversity in the various aspects of BEd and PGCE courses. In BEd courses, where there are more possibilities for innovation, some institutions have embarked upon interesting initiatives. PGCE courses with their limited provision for contact time have, perhaps predictably, been less successful, although some developments are taking place.

In the meantime, newly qualified teachers are likely to have a considerable variety of previous experience and background knowledge of multilingual Britain. Some training institutions are more successful than others in the approach to linguistic diversity. It would be unfortunate if selection for first teaching posts favoured applicants from a small group of training institutions. At present there is little evidence of this. However, as some authorities begin to be more rigorous in asking applicants to demonstrate a commitment to equal opportunities, this situation could arise. There is a strong case, as the Swann Committee argues, for expecting LEAs, through induction courses and INSET, to prepare teachers for specifically local needs. The danger that teacher trainers will abdicate responsibility to LEAs is quite real - when we are considering sensitive issues of ethnicity and prejudice. There is an urgent

1. 'Training for Linguistic Diversity' seminar organised by the LDIP project at the University of Nottingham, January 1988.

```
┌─────────────────────────────────────────────────────────────┐
│ AIMS IN WORKING WITH STUDENTS:                                │
│                                                               │
│    *    acquiring some basic knowledge about the linguistic   │
│         minorities of Britain                                 │
│    *    developing an awareness of all the languages that pupils │
│         use                                                   │
│    *    creating an awareness of the role of language in learning │
│         in educational and social contexts                    │
│    *    encouraging students to see bilingualism as an asset  │
│         rather than a problem                                 │
│    *    promoting an appreciation of the relationship between first │
│         and second language acquisition                       │
│    *    establishing an understanding of the wider context (e.g. │
│         language and power)                                    │
│    *    practical experience of multilingual schools          │
│                                                               │
│ IN TRAINING INSTITUTIONS:                                     │
│                                                               │
│    *    confront racist attitudes and overcome resistance to  │
│         change                                                │
│    *    employ more bilingual tutors and tutors from ethnic   │
│         minorities                                            │
│    *    review training materials and resources, and update   │
│    *    involve local communities, bilingual teachers and LEA │
│         INSET providers                                       │
└─────────────────────────────────────────────────────────────┘
```

Table 1 - *Recommendations from LDIP Training Seminar*

need to establish a division of labour which would help initial
trainers to design courses which offer appropriate experiences
for all teachers and local authorities to plan induction and in-
service training relevant to their particular circumstances.

Bilingual teachers

The Government paper *Teaching Quality* (HMSO, 1983) has
underlined the need to recruit more teachers from ethnic
minorities. Thinking in this area has been developed through
discussion stimulated by the publication of the Swann Report
(1986), which devotes part of a chapter to the subject. A
number of teacher training institutions have responded by taking
positive action to increase the number of black applicants. In
liaison with LEAs, secondary schools and careers advisory

services, through developing community links, and by creative publicity, some training institutions have begun to redress the imbalance in our teaching force. Where access courses to attract students have been established, the potential of such courses to attract students from the ethnic minorities has, in places, been harnessed. Until ethnic monitoring is fully implemented, however, no accurate information on the influence of these initiatives is available. When considering language issues it is not, of course, to be assumed that all black teachers will be bilingual. Similarly, not all bilingual teachers will consider themselves 'black'. Boosting black recruitment is, however, likely to increase the number of bilinguals in the teaching force, although it is important to bear in mind that not all bilingual students entering the teaching profession will want to focus their attention on language teaching. They may lack confidence in their own language skills or may not have developed a high enough level of literacy in their first language to consider teaching it, or their interest may lie elsewhere - in maths or science for instance.

Primary specialists may be more interested in class teaching or the work of a nursery unit than in the sometimes marginal existence of support teaching. Nevertheless, such teachers may have a vital contribution to make in developing and implementing a school's language policy.[*] At the secondary level many schools now realise how valuable bilingual teachers can be in enriching language awareness programmes, taster courses and other short-term language learning experiences. Bilingual teachers who do not claim to be specialists in community languages have an important role to play in this work.

Nonetheless, a coherent language policy cannot depend upon the goodwill of the 'non-specialist' bilingual teachers, just as it cannot depend upon voluntary or poorly paid ancillary help. The work of bilingual teachers should complement the specialism of community language teachers and create new possibilities for monolingual colleagues.

Community language teachers and course provision

It is at times difficult to separate the issues of teacher training

---

* In primary schools the potential for representing linguistic diversity in cross-curricular topic work is well documented (D Houlton, 1985; Gregory Woollard, 1985)

from curriculum organisation in schools. Indeed, there are those who would argue that such distinctions have repeatedly contributed to the mismatch between teacher preparation and the reality of life in classrooms. The lack of consensus in LEAs and schools about the position of community languages in the curriculum causes teacher trainers to tread warily.

Although the majority of educationists and practitioners involved now agree that the languages of ethnic minorities must not be allowed to remain in a marginal position in the school timetable, issues concerning the relationship between modern languages (in the established sense of the term) and modern minority languages have yet to be satisfactorily resolved. Controversy over the assessment of GCSE in Urdu and Panjabi is evidence of this uneasy relationship - can one in fact apply the same criteria for assessing the achievement of the monolingual English pupil who learns French as a foreign language at secondary school to that of the Panjabi/English bilingual who studies Urdu?

If the position of community languages in the modern language curriculum is uncertain at school level, a similar uncertainty is reflected in teacher training. Traditionally, modern language graduates have concentrated on the pedagogical aspects of their subject specialism. Training institutions generally assume that students' first degrees have equipped them with sufficient fluency in their chosen language, although, as Craft and Atkins (1983) point out, some PGCE courses allow students to 'brush-up' a language or even develop minimal competence in a new language. Since the number of degree courses in community languages is negligible, it is unlikely that the traditional PGCE route would be able to provide teachers to meet the growing demand.

British universities and other higher education institutions are beginning to extend their provision in response to a rising demand for language graduates, but there is still only a handful of institutions that offer advanced study in one of Britain's own community languages and only one that offers a degree in South-Asian languages. Although there is a tendency for language departments to offer more integrated degrees, none has yet explored the possibility of an integrated degree with a certificate of education. All in all, there is little room for optimism when considering the established PGCE route for the training of community language teachers. Neither is there much potential in the BEd route - BEd degrees with a specialism in modern language teaching are a rarity; those offering community languages non-existent.

It is in this rather gloomy climate that several institutions have attempted to break what Craft and Atkins (1983) call the 'vicious circle' of teacher supply by mounting special PGCE courses for community language teachers, usually in collaboration with a consortium of LEAs. Table 2 on page 138-139 gives an impression of some of these initiatives.

Those recruited to these courses have a wide variety of previous experience, but it is important to note that the majority have overseas qualifications. The principles underlying DES recognition for some community language teachers continue to be hotly debated and certainly at times the formal requirements seem like a maze of rules and regulations. Enabling those with overseas qualifications to achieve Qualified Teacher Status is an important short-term measure and these recent developments are a welcome initiative. However, there is little doubt that, in the long term, it is our capacity as an education system to produce graduates in community languages that is likely to be the decisive factor in the supply of community language teachers and, for that matter, for the whole future of these languages in the school curriculum. This applies not only to those South-Asian languages that have been referred to, but also to smaller linguistic minorities (such as Turkish or Gaelic for example).

The requirements of the National Curriculum will mean an expansion of language teaching in the secondary phase. Diversification in language learning is advocated in the recent DES paper 'Modern Languages in the School Curriculum' (DES, 1988). The part which community languages will play in this predicted expansion and diversification is as yet unclear. However, the need to boost the recruitment of language teachers is certainly pressing. Two recent Government proposals that may help to relieve the shortfall in the supply of community language teachers are worth considering. First, the suggestion that increased mobility and co-operation between the member states of the European community (after 1992) may be used to attract European trained language teachers; second, proposals for establishing a new grade of Licensed Teacher (LT).

The use of European-trained language teachers has considerable appeal. We would, for instance, be in a position to attract native speakers from the major European languages. This could add strength to the commonly taught languages such as French and German. More importantly, it opens the possibility of teaching a much wider range of languages including some, such as Italian or Greek, that are community languages in Britain.

Proposals for establishing the LT grade are also of considerable interest. Here recruitment could help to attract the thousands of teachers with overseas qualifications (particularly those from Southern Asia, the Middle East and Africa), who are put off from entering the profession by the difficulties of achieving QTS. LT's should be no substitute for qualified teachers. Given the right support as well as the opportunity to qualify, such an initiative might begin to tap the linguistic expertise of ethnic minority communities.

Perhaps it is timely to think about how we can train a greater variety of language teachers. This will inevitably call for some careful educational planning and the dismantling of those barriers that stand in the way of a true recognition of the linguistic resources of minority groups in Britain.

The corresponding decline in the supply of modern languages graduates entering teaching is worrying. Perhaps it is timely to think about how we can train a greater variety of language teachers. This will inevitably call for some careful educational planning, and the dismantling of those barriers that stand in the way of a true recognition of the linguistic resources of minority groups in Britain.

Conclusion

In conclusion I would like to suggest some key areas for future development. A unifying theme here is the need to give all language and dialects equal status in the education system. This is based on the evidence that most linguistic minorities in Britain experience a lack of bargaining power, combined with a belief that education can take an active part in removing these inequalities.

1.   INITIAL TRAINING INSTITUTIONS

-   Need to focus work on linguistic diversity for all teachers. This should be done in the full knowledge of the capability of LEAs to offer specific induction and INSET courses.

-   Need to boost the recruitment of ethnic minority teachers in general - bilinguals in particular.

Table 2: SOME INITIATIVES IN THE TRAINING OF BILINGUAL TEACHERS
(This is based on information available to the author at the time of publication)

	Qualification	Course Type	Target	DES Quota	Participating LEAs	Broad Objectives	Principle languages catered for
Birmingham Polytechnic	PGCE (secondary)	1 yr full-time	Mature bilinguals	5 out of 25 places for modern languages	Birmingham	Competent teachers to respond to needs of local bilingual pupils	Punjabi and Urdu
Leeds Polytechnic	PGCE (primary)	2 yrs part-time	Mature bilinguals with overseas qualifications	15	Leeds	Class teachers who can work as bilingual specialists	Urdu and other 5 Asian languages
University of Manchester	PGCE (primary)	2 yrs part-time	Bilingual assistants - some with overseas qualifications	15	Manchester Bolton Tameside Oldham	Class teachers with a specialism in bilingualism	5 Asian languages

Thames Polytechnic	PGCE (secondary)	1 yr full-time	Modern language graduates and bilinguals with overseas qualifications	33	ILEA	Bilingual specialists who can work across the curriculum	Bengali, Turkish, Chinese
University of London Institute of Education	PGCE (primary and secondary)	1 yr part-time (as part of full course)	Bilingual instructor and teacher in LEAs lacking QTS	not agreed	links with several	Specialist subject teacher with a further professional option to teach a community language	Gujarati, Spanish, Polish, Urdu +
Polytechnic of North London	PGCE (primary)	1 yr full-time; 2 yrs part-time	Mature bilinguals	17 full-time; 20 part-time	informal links with several	Good primary teacher with specialisation in multilingual education	Greek, Turkish, South-Asian

- Need to expand short-term measures designed to give Qualified Teacher Status to Community Language Teachers (some of whom may already have a qualification that is not recognised by the DES). Although many such teachers are already employed by LEAs, there is still a need for some active recruitment.

- Long-term planning involves co-operation with Higher Education departments who have not traditionally been concerned with teacher training. Language Departments are an obvious target. We need to remove the structural barriers that currently prevent the legitimate study of community languages in their own right.

2.   SCHOOLS AND LEAs

- Schools and LEAs have an important contribution to make by reviewing their language policies in the light of current thinking about linguistic diversity. The diversity of language experiences in pupils and society at large should be a cornerstone in such policy development.

- Developing language policies will help to reveal the need in terms of suitably qualified and specialist teachers. Consequent changes in staff appointment criteria would help to create more career opportunities for ethnic minority teachers.

- Black and bilingual teachers need to be given power and status in LEAs and schools and should be encouraged to take a central role in decision making.

- Bilingual teachers need incentives to take on this challenging task and require support both from within institutions and from external agencies.

REFERENCES

Arora, R. *Initial teacher training in multicultural education: towards good practice.* (1986) London: Routledge and Kegan Paul.

The accreditation of achievement across languages in the secondary phase

John Broadbent

The measurement of linguistic performance has proved to be a minefield for teachers, examination boards, and for the various government agencies which have been established in recent years with a brief to monitor standards. Equally problematical, from the point of view of the pupil in the secondary school, are the criteria according to which it may be possible for a learner to become more aware of his or her own progress. In the context of moves to establish the equivalence of qualifications across Europe and beyond, there is now a heightened urgency about the search for more relevant ways of describing - and enhancing - multilingual skills.

Taking examples from the Canadian context, Cummins (1984) has drawn attention to the dangers inherent in the assumptions underlying the measurement of academic progress as far as bilingual pupils are concerned. In Britain, regrettably, the general educational concern to emphasise those skills which pupils are able and willing to perform has rarely been stretched sufficiently to record their abilities in the languages and dialects which they bring from their local community. Some sections of Bullock (1975) discuss this, but the use of the singular in the title - *A language for life* - gives more than a clue to the monolingual perspective permeating this report. Improvements in techniques for assessing and describing skills in the use of English were consolidated by the report, and these improvements are still reflected in the techniques developed for the most recent English examinations.

The current work on attainment targets and testing arrangements, as envisaged by the 1988 Education Reform Act in England and Wales for pupils aged seven and eleven, does take some account of skills in languages other than the medium of instruction itself. Sections of the Report of the Task Group on Assessment and Testing (DES, 1988), and of the subsequent documents on Maths, Science and English, in referring to the setting of clear objectives achievable by the full ability range, have drawn attention to the value of using mother tongues other than English. These references are, however, placed beside arguments about the possibility of the exemption of pupils with

141

poor skills in English. If the pupil's home language does come to be seen as necessary for formative assessment, clearly that same language will also be relevant for further cognitive growth. The National Curriculum for the secondary phase does envisage the recording of skills in languages other than English at the ages of fourteen and sixteen, but principally for *a modern foreign language specified in an order of the Secretary of State*, and *in relation to schools in Wales which are not Welsh-speaking schools, Welsh.* There is a declared intention to accommodate the local enterprise of teachers in the forms of assessment eventually to be adopted, but it remains to be seen to what extent the different methodologies currently used in end-of-term examinations and school-based systems of profiling can be related to each other without losing their essential independence, teacher control and consequently their greater relevance to different constituencies of students. It would certainly appear that local education authorities and schools at the present are succeeding in working out local schemes which by and large are meeting with approval from the examining consortia on which the Government will have to rely for accreditation. The battle for bilingual assessment is not lost.

Towards improved descriptions of linguistic performance

Summative types of assessment, such as have been made available by school examining boards, or which have been developed by educational researchers to prove this or that hypothesis, have on the whole failed to capture the elements involved in the successful use of more than one language. Schools Council (1983) spelled out the dangers of applying assessment techniques evolved for foreign languages to the languages which are in daily use in a wide range of different communities in England today, whilst Rosen (1982), on the other hand, is devastating in his assault on the inadequacies of the methods developed by the Assessment of Performance Unit for evaluating the competences of speakers of English as a mother tongue and as a second language.

More recently, however, arguments have come to the fore which seek to reduce the resultant wastage of potential, and which would seem to offer more positive uses for analyses of linguistic attainment. Perhaps the most significant shift has been towards criterion-referencing, towards descriptions of performance which have an intrinsic face validity without being tied to statistical norms. Such descriptions can help to create a clear impression for learners of the ways in which their performance itself is actually improving, especially in classrooms where pupils are encouraged to comment constructively on one another's work. Such opportunities for the comparison of performance could result in the formulation and adoption by the learners of clear criteria for excellence in terms of communication. It is quite possible that the formative types of assessment which now seem to be preferred in professional circles will be easier to develop in relation to bilingual pupils, since such learners at least have some internal points of comparison which can be related to their proficiency across more than one language.

As evidenced by the general examining criteria described in DES (1985), complementary initiatives claim to be based on strategies which can highlight what pupils are able to do, rather than what they cannot do; where evaluation does reveal shortcomings in performance, it is sometimes asserted that assessment techniques can be used to highlight areas of difficulty which can subsequently be remedied. The underlying philosophical stances have found their way into the assessment of linguistic performance, although in somewhat different forms, depending on whether one is analysing performance in English as a mother tongue, or in a language which has been acquired in later life.

From the studies that have been conducted to date it does seem unlikely that any 'absolute standards' can be invented of the kind referred to by the Secretary of State for Education in speeches during 1984, at the height of the campaigns to present the new unified system of examining which was called the General Certificate of Secondary Education (GCSE). There is nevertheless considerable scope for closer observation and analysis of performance amongst bilingual learners: drawing on the work of Patel (reported in Reid, 1984) the Community Languages in the Secondary Curriculum Project (1987) was able to develop various versions of a bilingual self-assessment questionnaire. A framework for language assignments was then constructed.

There remains much work to be done in this field. Various forms of school certification have become available in recent years - records of achievement, awards for progress within a series of graded objectives, new school-leaving examinations at 16 +, and a wide range of more specialised qualifications, both vocational and academic. In some schools, different permutations of all five forms of certification, as described in greater detail below, are being developed simultaneously, often within a single subject area. Teachers of modern foreign languages, for example, have found that graded objectives can lead very easily into the idea of regular assessment and into greater pupil involvement: work on piloting modular courses towards the new General Certificate of Secondary Education or equally towards the Certificate of Pre-Vocational Education have been felt to have fitted well with profiling for Records of Achievement.

Accreditation of achievement in community languages

Research referred to in Taylor and Hegarty (1985) suggests that there is a strong desire on the part of families using community languages to ensure that their children are entered for public examinations in the relevant languages as used at home. In *Assessment in a Multicultural Society: Community Languages at 16+* (Schools Council, 1983), the report drew attention to the fact that the format still in use at that time for GCE papers in South-Asian languages was created to help universities to discover whether overseas candidates possessed suitable skills to follow a degree course: the principal skill required was the use of an academic variety of English.

Fortunately, the argument and recommendations in the Report were sufficiently convincing to influence a number of the new initiatives already being taken by local education authorities and examining bodies for pupils in the compulsory years of secondary schooling. These initiatives have included Graded Objectives, the Certificate of Pre-Vocational Education, a variety of vocational qualifications, especially the Bilingual Skills Certificate of the Institute of Linguists, the General Certificate of Secondary Education and Records of Achievement: in turn each is considered below for its potential contribution to the validation of linguistic skills already present in the school population.

Graded objectives

The contribution of the vocational examining bodies will not be discussed here, as although they have some relevance for schools, their main emphasis is at the post-16 level, where bodies such as the LCCI, Institute of Linguists and BTEC have been making provision for testing community languages (JBPVE, 1985, Institute of Linguists, 1986).

The idea of organising a communicative teaching syllabus in terms of a series of steps which could be attempted by all learners regardless of their linguistic background was first espoused by teachers of French and German in the United Kingdom. Amin, Broadbent and Mehta (1985) have attempted to apply the basic principles of graded objectives for foreign language learning to the languages present in different localities throughout the United Kingdom. These principles, with their special emphases on the recording of positive achievement, on task and syllabus definition in terms of communicative competence, on negotiation and on continuous assessment had been developed in opposition to the kinds of 16 + examinations being proposed in the early seventies. Through the graded objectives approach, linguistic performance is seen to be measurable in its elementary stages, at least for the most predictable transactions. Tests have consequently been devised to list in some detail exactly what a beginning learner can be expected to do. Assessment here has as its goal a description of successfully performed tasks such as 'introducing oneself' or 'buying food and drink in a shop'. Subsequent developments, including developments in a wide range of community languages, are very fully documented in Page and Hewett (1988). In general, it seems fair to say that the kinds of tests which are used to check success in a series of graded objectives in the early stages of learning a language for transactional purposes, can hardly be applied to the more reflective kinds of expression which call upon inner resources and on which more fluent users of a particular language may be encouraged to deploy their skills.

Graded assessment

The possibility of achieving GCSE by a process of continuous assessment is one which is welcomed by many teachers and pupils. The London and East Anglian Group for GCSE Examinations (LEAG) has been developing such a scheme (Graded Assessment in Modern Languages, London - GAMLL) initially for use in the assessment of French and Urdu. Now parallel developments are taking place in Spanish, German and Italian. The development phase started in 1985 and, it is hoped, will finish with the necessary approval in 1989. This would mean that certain of the Graded Assessment levels would be counted as equivalent to the GCSE grades A-G. Pupils would be able to work through the Graded Assessment levels at their own pace, receiving LEAG Statements of Achievement at appropriate points and a GCSE certificate, where the level justified it. No end-of-course examination would be required.

In common with Graded Objectives schemes in languages, Graded Assessment involves a carefully researched list of criteria, related to a number of levels of performance. This allows the scheme to be flexible and progressive, and it has been planned to fit in with the commonly available coursebooks in languages.

In some contrast to Graded Objectives schemes, Graded Assessment seeks to integrate the assessment of pupils into the lesson time, without requiring special testing occasions. This means that the teacher is not faced with the need to plan lessons around the testing arrangements. The pupils are also able to be assessed at the point when they are ready and do not really have to be tested on one occasion.

The pilot scheme is proving to be highly motivating for pupils. Teachers, too, are finding that the extra record-keeping that is required is less of a burden as time goes on and that Graded Assessment records provide very helpful material for other new assessment initiatives. Records of Achievement is one such area: it is possible to use the statements listed in Graded Assessment as a basis for writing pupil profiles.

The General Certificate of Secondary Education (GCSE)

The framework for the GCSE has evolved from a combination of the Ordinary Level of the General Certificate of Education (GCE 'O' level) with the Certificate of Secondary Education (CSE) and embodies the key concept that linguistic performance is based on 'successful communication', not 'grammatical accuracy', 'native speaker proficiency' or 'range of vocabulary'. General criteria governing all syllabuses and assessment procedures for GCSE examinations were approved in January 1985, together with specific criteria for examinations in English, French, Welsh and seventeen other (non-language) subjects. The new examination was first administered in summer 1988. Syllabuses in all subjects, including community languages, were subject to approval and monitoring by the Secondary Examinations Council (SEC). (This body has now been replaced by a statutory body, the School Examinations and Assessment Council (SEAC), which inherits a number of problems which arise from the direct transfer of specifications for French examinations to community languages.) A working conference held by the SEC in conjunction with the DES and HMI in May 1988 suggested a number of possible approaches which could form part of an amended set of criteria, based on existing criteria, but different from the criteria for French, and to be called 'National Criteria for Languages' (SEC, 1988).

In contrast with those currently obtaining for foreign languages, the aims, methods of teaching, and settings for use are all different for languages in local use, and do not need to be predicated on the needs of a visitor to the original language area. Serious doubts have therefore been raised as to whether papers in a language spoken by students at home should follow the same model as foreign languages, where fluency is traditionally less highly rewarded than accuracy. There are calls to abolish the role-play exercises: these require the candidates to adhere strictly to a brief provided in English, and to avoid embellishing the conversational exchanges with their own originality. There is also a strongly supported call for methods of assessment which place less reliance on the candidates' knowledge of English. The Midland Examining Group and the London and East Anglian Group have now arranged for the rubrics of their listening exercises to be provided both in English and in the language of the examination: candidates will be able to answer the comprehension questions in either language.

The General Criteria for the GCSE as published by the Secondary Examinations Council recommended that part of the assessment should be school-based. Procedures involving written or tape-recorded coursework could therefore form a very important part of a GCSE examination in a community language, since such coursework offers so much scope for different levels of attainment. The Mode 1 papers in community languages which have so far been devised do not include coursework, however: it has fallen to individual schools submitting Mode 3 proposals to develop the full potential of the new system of examinations. One way forward is suggested by Mode 2 papers in History which have been prepared for schools in the Inner London Education Authority; these make it viable for a school to submit work in a pupil's first language, provided that the teachers assessing the work can demonstrate adequate procedures for standardising assignments. The potential for teaching and assessing components of the foundation subjects specified by the National Curriculum through the medium of a wide range of languages is real and exciting.

Comparable records of achievement

The Department of Education and Science (1987) recognises that many important attainments are not reflected in examination results. The Government's objective is said to be to establish national arrangements for Records of Achievement for all school-leavers in England and Wales by 1990. It has funded a number of pilot schemes prior to drawing up national guidelines. The National Council for Vocational Qualifications has concerned itself with the need to establish comparability of qualifications within Britain, and across national boundaries, especially in preparation for Europe of 1992.

General criteria, however, have yet to be devised which could establish a basis for comparing various levels of attainment in a wide range of modern languages (including community languages) as identified by the GCSE, by the various vocational qualifications on offer and by the wide range of graded test schemes available. The Northern Partnership for Records of Achievement (1987) has suggested that progress in language learning can be assessed along broadly comparable lines if raw marks are adjusted to take account of factors like **predictability, independence,** and **refinement.** If these suggestions are developed a little further, **predictability** can perhaps be taken to include:

1. the number and range of learning experiences and assignments in which each individual pupil has been actively involved ...

2. the extent to which the language which the learner is expected to absorb and use has been rehearsed; how much it conforms to set patterns; how much it is supported by contextual clues ...

Independence would involve some measures of

3. the level, and kind of support offered to the pupil both inside and outside the classroom in accomplishing the tasks required by the syllabus ...

4. the levels of creativity displayed by the learner, which relate closely to the extent to which a pupil is expected to take the initiative and to make his/her own unique contribution...

Refinement in the context of bilingual learners would suggest the extent to which the student was able to purify out the various sources of his or her language under circumstances of code-switching, and more generally

5. the levels of refinement, precision and clarification of language which the learner is expected either to initiate or comprehend...

Social Interaction would take account of, for example,

6. the level of self-confidence and social ease displayed by the learner in making, developing and maintaining contact with an audience, and indeed in all forms of classroom interaction with peers.

In the long term, the assessment of linguistic attainment as a whole has much to gain from close study of performance in bilingual learners, but to date there has been little recognition of this. There is value in comparing levels of linguistic performance in different contexts, so as to establish relative descriptions of educational attainment. Such an enterprise is not only desirable in Britain's multilingual society; more importantly, the hopes for greater mobility for workers across Europe and beyond demand more urgently than ever that equivalences be found for the qualifications awarded by a whole range of educational institutions across the world.

SELECT BIBLIOGRAPHY

Amin, S, J Broadbent, and M Mehta. (1985). *Graded objectives, graded tests and 16+ examinations for community languages.* National Council for Mother Tongue Teaching.

Bullock, A. (1975). A *language for life*. Report of the Committee of Inquiry. London: HMSO.

Cummins, J. (1984). *Bilingualism and special education: issues in assessment and pedagogy*. Clevedon, Avon: Multilingual Matters.

Department of Education and Science. (1985). *GCSE general criteria*. London: HMSO.

Department of Education and Science. (1987a). *Examination reform for schools: a guide for employers to recent changes in the schools examination and assessment system*. London: HMSO.

Department of Education and Science. (1987b). *The National Curriculum 5 - 16: a consultation document*. London: DES.

Department of Education and Science. (1988). *National Curriculum Task Group on Assessment and Testing: a report*. London: DES, Cardiff: Welsh Office.

Her Majesty's Inspectorate. (1977). Matters for discussion 3: *Modern languages in comprehensive schools*. London: HMSO.

Institute of Linguists. (1986). *Bilingual Skills Certificate*. London: Institute of Linguists Educational Trust.

Joint Board of Pre-Vocational Education. (1985). *The Certificate of Pre-Vocational Education: framework and criteria for approval of schemes*. JBPVE.

Linguistic Minorities Project. (1983.) *Linguistic minorities in England: a report from the linguistic minorities project*. London: University of London Institute of Education; Redhill: Tinga Tinga.

Linguistic Minorities Project. (1985). *The other languages of England*. London: Routledge and Kegan Paul.

London Chamber of Commerce and Industry. (1982). *Commercial education scheme: languages for industry and commerce*. Sidcup: LCCI Examinations Board.

Marland, M. (1987). *Multilingual Britain*. London: CILT.

Miller, J. (1983). *Many voices*. London: Routledge and Kegan Paul.

Norrish, J. (1983). *Language learners and their errors*. London: Macmillan.

Northern Partnership for Records of Achievement (NPRA)/Northern Examining Association. (1987): *Pilot scheme in the accreditation of graded test schemes in modern languages*, January 1987-January 1988: *Criteria for accreditation*: 1987. London: HMSO.

Orr, L. and Nuttall, D L. (1983). *Determining standards in the proposed single system of examining at 16-plus*. Comparability in Examinations Occasional Paper 2. London: Schools Council.

Patel, H. (1981). *Teaching Gujarati at Alperton High School* in Reid, E. (ed) (1984).

Reid, E. (ed). (1984). *Minority community languages in school*. London: CILT. (NCLE Papers and Reports 4)

Rosen, H. and Burgess, T. (1980). *Languages and dialects of London school children*. London: Ward Lock.

Rosen, H. (1982). *The language monitors*. London: University of London Institute of Education. (Bedford Way Papers).

Secondary Examinations Council. (1985). *Coursework assessment in the GCSE*. London: SEC.

Schools Council. (1983). *Assessment in a multicultural society: community languages at 16+*. York: Longman.

Swann, Lord. (Chairman). (1985). *Education for all*. Report of the Committee of Inquiry into the Education of Children from Ethnic Minority Groups. London: HMSO.

Taylor, M J with S Hegarty. (1985). *The best of both worlds?* Windsor: NFER-Nelson.

Tosi, A. (1979). *Bilinguismo, transfert e interferenze: consideraziome sul processo di acquisizione dell' italiano in figli di emigrati bilingui in inglese e dialetto campano*. Atti de Congresso, Societa di Linguistica Italiana.

Van Ek, J. (1976). *The threshold level for modern language learning in schools*. Longman/Council of Europe.

Wright, J. (1982). *Bilingualism in education*. London: Issues in Race and Education Collective.

Afterword

The Education (National Curriculum) Modern Foreign Language
Order 1989

The debate on the education of bilingual members of the ethnic
minority communities has come to one of its periodic crossroads,
and been given new urgency by the government's statutory order
and circular on modern foreign languages in the National
Curriculum in May 1989 on which languages should have
priority of introduction into the schools. Schools are required to
offer pupils the opportunity to study at least one of the working
languages of the European Community (named in Schedule One
of the Order): Danish, Dutch, French, German, Modern Greek,
Italian, Portuguese, Spanish. Pupils may pick a language for
their foundation subject from a group of non-EC languages
(Schedule Two) - Arabic, Bengali, Mandarin or Cantonese
Chinese, Gujarati, Modern Hebrew, Hindi, Japanese, Panjabi,
Russian, Turkish and Urdu - provided they have already been
given the option to study an EC language. The lines have thus
not been drawn on educational or even economic grounds, and
this has blurred the picture somewhat, since in British terms
there is an overlap: some of the languages which are British
community languages (Greek, Italian, Portuguese, Spanish), have
received seemingly 'favoured' treatment by being included in
Schedule One; others are named in Schedule Two. Of these
latter, only Japanese and Russian are not significant in British
community language terms. Schools have always been able to
offer any language, provided they have the resources and the
community and parental backing to teach them. The government
order does not contradict this, although it perhaps makes the
framework of provision more restricted. Nevertheless, the
formality of naming the languages does perhaps provide a peg on
which community languages may hang a claim for a natural place
in the mainstream curriculum, if not as the first or only foreign
language, at least as one of two.

Some teachers and advisers have argued that the use of two
lists tends to accord privilege to European languages in a way
that reflects rather a narrow view of European interests, both
economic and social, and that it is possible that under LMS
(Local Management of Schools) and opting-out arrangements,
governing bodies may be under pressure to take decisions on

which languages shall be incorporated in the curriculum on financial rather than pedagogical, educational or community-based (socio-cultural) grounds. There is also the psychological effect of putting forward two lists of languages rather than one undifferentiated one. Schedule Two languages may come to be seen as the 'second eleven', thus negating some of the value of being named at all. Those parents not convinced of the value of multicultural approaches within education may see differentiated lists as reinforcement for their ideas; parents from the communities, on the other hand, may exert greater pressure to establish their own schools, thus continuing a process of marginalisation of their languages vis-à-vis the mainstream. Given the importance of parent-governors and the value of home-school links, therefore, more attention should be paid to ways of helping parents to understand the education issues involved, with particular reference to cultural diversity and the values appropriate to the creation of a true pluralist society.

There is an irony, however, in the lack of provision for language teaching in the primary school, which will have the paradoxical effect of turning children who were either bilingual, or potentially bilingual, when they entered primary school into monolinguals, and of causing possible difficulties at secondary school level (when language learning is officially smiled upon). Although not all will wish to study their heritage tongue as a foreign language, the needless loss of a skill is always a cause for regret. In the case of community languages, therefore, there is a need for substantial language learning activity at primary level, to which children with English as mother tongue should be admitted. Such a programme would be in addition to any language awareness programmes and might most usefully be introduced through, for example, topic work carried out largely through the target language.

Meanwhile, two of Christopher Brumfit's language education components may be singled out: the idea of the development of knowledge of the nature of language in a multilingual society; and the development of fairly extensive practical competence in at least one language other than one's own. The first is reinforced by the Cox and Kingman Reports, which emphasise the importance of forms of language awareness in the curriculum. Among the implications of the second is the recognition that the concerns of bilingual children call for concentration on the needs of young people as developing communicators in a multilingual environment; this implies working relations across curricular frontiers. Some approaches are illustrated by Laurie Kershook, and by the case studies in this volume. These are only four studies, however; there is a need for further careful ethnographic studies of the use of linguistic diversity across the curriculum of British schools.

Implementation of the language teaching proposals of the national curriculum raises other issues. The issue of diversification of language learning has highlighted a number of problems of resourcing, especially of training or re-training the large number of teachers who will be required to implement the study of two foreign languages in the secondary years.

Many of the issues raised at the 1986 conference remain high on the agenda, and in particular we need to investigate ways of providing language training other than the single five-year course; to review teacher resources and linguistic competence; and, for community languages, career prospects; to harmonise systems of profiling and examinations. None of these concerns, of course, is intended to pre-empt the importance of English, but they are issues on which those involved with community languages should ensure that their voice is heard - a realistic possibility for the future, as LEA advisers both for English and for modern languages increasingly accept and exercise care for community languages, recognising that these languages can enrich the curriculum and the socio-cultural environment of a school.

In a field - the management of bilingualism in education - still too undeveloped to have cast-iron standards, this book is intended to shed light on the balance between theory and suggested practice, set against Government policy. It constitutes a statement of the theoretical position in favour of institutional support of a language policy for bilingualism, and indicates a route from policy to curriculum development.

The book is thus a contribution to the debate on the status and direction of Britain as a multilingual, multicultural society, expressed through the provisions of its education system. HMI (1983) have already noted that pupils ... *face the common experience of living in a world which is increasingly international, multi-ethnic and interdependent both economically and politically*, and acceptance of this must have an effect in school provision.

Within this understanding let us hope that community languages may find a natural place in the curriculum.

Bibliography

Adams, C. (ed). (1987). *Across seven seas and thirteen rivers: life stories of pioneer Sylheti settlers in Britain.* London: THAP.

Amin, S, J Broadbent, and M Mehta. (1985). *Graded objectives, graded tests and 16 + examinations for community languages.* National Council for Mother Tongue Teaching.

Arora, R. (1986). Initial teacher training. In: *Multicultural education - towards good practice.* London: Routledge and Kegan Paul.

Atkins, M J. (1985). Minority community languages: problems, strategies and issues for teacher educators. In *British Journal of Educational Studies*, vol 33, no 1, Feb. 1985.

Baldwin, T. (1983). *Teaching materials for Italian.* London: CILT.

Barnes, D. (1976). *From communication to curriculum.* Harmondsworth: Penguin.

Britton, J. (1970). *Language and learning.* London: Allen Lane.

Brumfit, C J and K Johnson, (eds). (1979). *The communicative approach to language teaching.* Oxford, London: Oxford University Press.

Bullock, A. (1975). *A language for life.* Report of the Committee of Inquiry. London: HMSO.

Community Languages in the Secondary Curriculum. J Broadbent. (Coordinator). (1987). *The inclusion of community languages in the normal curricular arrangements of local education authority maintained schools in England and Wales.* Report of the EC Pilot Project. (1984-87). London: University of London Institute of Education (Centre for Multicultural Education).

Cox, B. (Chairman). (1988). *English for ages 5 to 11.* London: National Curriculum Council.

Craft, M and M J Atkins. (1983). *Training teachers of ethnic minority community languages.* Nottingham: School of Education, University of Nottingham.

Cummins, J. (1984). *Bilingualism and special education: issues in assessment and pedagogy.* Clevedon, Avon: Multilingual Matters.

Department of Education and Science. (1983). *Foreign languages in the school curriculum: a consultative paper.* London: DES, Cardiff: Welsh Office.

Department of Education and Science. (1983). *Teaching quality.* London: HMSO.

Department of Education and Science. (1984). *Initial teacher training: approval of courses.* Circular 3/84. London: DES.

Department of Education and Science. (1985). *GCSE general criteria.* London: HMSO.

Department of Education and Science. (1987). *Examination reform for schools: a guide for employers to recent changes in the schools examination and assessment system.* London: HMSO.

Department of Education and Science. (1987). *The National Curriculum 5 - 16: a consultation document.* London: DES.

Department of Education and Science. (1988). *Education Reform Act.* London: HMSO.

Department of Education and Science. (1988). *Modern languages in the school curriculum.* London: HMSO.

Department of Education and Science. (1988). *National Curriculum Task Group on Assessment and Testing: a report.* London: DES, Cardiff: Welsh Office.

Donmall, B G. (1985). *Language awareness.* London: CILT. (NCLE papers and reports).

Great Britain. Parliament. House of Commons Home Affairs Committee (GB. P. H. of C. HAC.) *Chinese community in*

Britain. Second Report from the Home Affairs Committee, Session 1984-5. Vol. 1: Report and Proceedings of the Committee; Vol. 2: Minutes of evidence; Vol. 3: Appendices. London: HMSO, 1985.

Griffiths, J. (ed). (1982). *Asian links.* Record of a broadcast series. London: Commission For Racial Equality.

Hargreaves, D H. (1984). *Improving secondary schools.* London: ILEA.

Her Majesty's Inspectorate. (1977). *Modern languages in comprehensive schools.* London: HMSO. (Department of Education and Science. HMI series: Matters for Discussion 3).

Her Majesty's Inspectorate. (1983). *Curriculum 11-16: towards a statement of entitlement.* London: HMSO for Department of Education and Science.

Her Majesty's Inspectorate. (1984). *Mother tongue teaching in school and community: an HMI Enquiry in four LEAs.* London: HMSO.

Her Majesty's Inspectorate. (1986). *English from 5 to 16.* London: HMSO.

Her Majesty's Inspectorate. (1987). *Modern foreign languages to 16.* London: HMSO. (Department of Education and Science. HMI series: Curriculum Matters 8).

Hornsey, A. (1986). Modern and community languages - convergence or divergence? *Bulletin.* ILEA Languages Centre.[1]

Houlton, D. (1985). *All our languages.* London: Edward Arnold.

Inner London Education Authority English Centre. (1985). *The island.* London: ILEA.

Inner London Education Authority. *Books in Bengali*: T Rehman, et al. (Comps). (1987). London: ILEA.

1. The plan was then more radical and not constrained by National Curriculum proposals.

Khan, V S. (1985). *Language education for all?*. Swann Report, Chapter 7, London: University of London Institute of Education.

Kingman, Sir J. (Chairman). (1988). *Report of the Committee of Inquiry into the Teaching of English Language.* London: HMSO for Department of Education and Science.

Lepschy, A L and G Lepschy. (1977). *The Italian language today.* London: Hutchinson.

Linguistic Minorities Project. (1983). *Linguistic minorities in England: a report from the Linguistic Minorities Project.* London: University of London Institute of Education; Redhill: Tinga Tinga.

Linguistic Minorities Project. (1985). *The other languages of England.* London: Routledge and Kegan Paul.

Littlewood, W T. (1981). *Communicative language teaching.* Cambridge: Cambridge University Press.

Marland, M. (1987). *Multilingual Britain.* London: CILT.

Merchant, G. (1987). *Progress Report - 2.* Nottingham: University of Nottingham, Linguistic Diversity in the Primary School Project.

Mitchell, R, and others. (1987). *Report of an independent evaluation of the Western Isles' Bilingual Education Project.* Stirling: University of Stirling, Department of Education.

Molteno, M. (1986). *Teaching Britain's community languages: materials and methods.* With examples from Urdu. London: CILT.

National Children's Centre. (1984). *'The silent minority'*. The Report of the Fourth National Conference on the Chinese community in Great Britain. (November 1982). Huddersfield: NCC.

Page, B and D Hewett. (1987). *Languages step by step: graded objectives in the UK.* London: CILT.

Palermo, D S, and others. (1956). The relationship of anxiety in children to performance in a complex learning task. *Child Development*, vol 27, no 3, pp. 333-337.

Quaker Community Relations Committee (QCRC). (1981). *The Chinese in Britain today*. Report of Conference, (1981). London: Commission For Racial Equality.

Raleigh, M. (1981). The *languages book*. London: ILEA English Centre.

Ranger, C. (1988). *Ethnic minority school teachers*. London: Commission for Racial Equality.

Reid, E. (ed). (1984). *Minority community languages in school*. London: CILT. (NCLE Papers and Reports 4).

Rosen, H. (1982). The *language monitors*. London: University of London Institute of Education. (Bedford Way Papers).

Sarason, S B, and others. (1960). *Anxiety in elementary school children*. New York: John Wiley and Sons.

Schools Council. (1983). *Assessment in a multicultural society: community languages at 16+*. York: Longman.

Secondary Examinations Council. (1988). *Community languages: assessment at 16+*. Report of a SEC/DES/HMI Working Conference, May 1988. London: SEC, 1988.

Stubbs, M. (1976). *Language, schools and classrooms*. London: Methuen.

Swann, Lord. (Chairman) (1985). *Education for all*. Report of the Committee of Inquiry into the Education of Children from Ethnic Minority Groups. London: HMSO.

Taylor, M J with S Hegarty. (1985). *The best of both worlds?* Windsor: NFER-Nelson.

Tosi, A. (1984). *Immigration and bilingual education*. Oxford: Pergamon Press.

Trudgill, P. (1975). *Accent, dialect and school*. London: Edward Arnold.

Wells, G. (1981). *Learning through interaction*. Cambridge: Cambridge University Press.

Wells, G, and J Nicholls. (1985). *Language and learning: an interactional perspective*. London: Falmer Press.

Biographies

JOHN BROADBENT

John Broadbent is an experienced teacher of English and French at primary level, English, French and German at secondary schools, and English for Specific Purposes to adults. He coordinated the project which brought Gujarati to the curriculum of Alperton High School, and was also coordinator of the EC Pilot Project: Community Languages in the Secondary Curriculum, 1984-1987.

CHRISTOPHER BRUMFIT

Christopher Brumfit is Professor of Education, with particular reference to language and linguistics in education, and Head of the Department of Education at the University of Southampton. He has a B.A. in Literature from Oxford, an M.A. in Applied Linguistics from Essex, and a PH.D. from London, and trained as a teacher at Makerere College, University of East Africa. He has also taught in primary and secondary schools in Britain and Africa, in a teacher training college in Brimingham, and in the Universities of Dar es Salaam and London. He has spent periods of several months working In India, China and Canada, and visited most parts of the world on short assignments. He has published nineteen books on ELT, literature teaching, and language in education.

BRUNO CERVI

Bruno Cervi, after fifteen years' involvement with education in Italy was assigned, in 1979, to the Education Department of the Italian Consulate General in London. He has been involved, both as teacher and coordinator with the teaching of Italian language and culture to children of Italian immigrants. He has carried out research on bilingual development, multicultural education and needs analysis of children of Italian origin, and took part in the E.C. Pilot Project: Community Languages in the Secondary Curriculum (1984-87) as coordinator of the team of consulate-sponsored teachers of Italian as a community language, operating in mainstream schools.

MONA GABB

Mrs Mona Gabb works for Surrey County Council as Head of Language Support Service based in Woking. Previously she was team leader (Maidenhead) in Language Support Service Berkshire. While working for Berkshire County she was involved with and helped Audrey Gregory and Norah Woollard produce *Talking and telling* and *Looking into language diversity in the classroom*.

ALAN HORNSEY

Alan Hornsey is a Senior Lecturer in Education and Head of Modern Languages at the Institute of Education, University of London. His research and teaching interests lie primarily in the field of modern language teaching in schools. He is the author of several books and articles in this area as well as in the study of modern German literature. His activities have included a period as president of the Association of Teachers of German, chairman of the standing committee of the National Council for Languages in Education and chairman of the languages advisory committee of the Royal Society of Arts Examinations Board.

BRYDEN KEENAN

Bryden Keenan has been Foreign Languages Adviser in Bedfordshire since 1975 and has been responsible for community languages since 1981 - at his own request and before such a step was recommended by the Swann Committee. He was previously a head of modern languages for ten years and taught in Coventry, Chiswick and Bracknell.

DIANE KENT

Diana Kent is a part-time teacher of textiles in several ILEA schools. Her interest in minority languages in school is reflected in her academic background which includes an Honours Psychology degree and Diploma in Education.

LAURIE KERSHOOK

Laurie Kershook is Advisory Teacher for Foreign Modern Languages in Haringey. Previously, as Head of Languages in a multilingual Haringey secondary school, he chaired a standing working party on bilingualism, initiated a Language Awareness course and a range of community languages options, and collaborated with colleagues on a variety of initiatives with a range of language curriculum objectives. He is a member of a group which is working towards the formation of a borough language policy for Haringey schools.

KEITH KIRBY

Keith Kirby has taught English, French, EFL and Drama, mainly in secondary schools but also in primary schools and colleges. Subsequently he served as a General Inspector for Ealing LEA where he was concerned with all aspects of language teaching and worked in many multilingual schools. From 1984 he was principal professional officer of the School Curriculum Development Committee (SCDC), for which his subject responsibilities included English and foreign languages. On behalf of SCDC, he established a number of major curriculum development projects including the National Writing Project and the National Oracy Project. He now works as an independent educational consultant.

STELLA LEWIS

Stella Lewis has worked for several years as a teacher of EFL and with pupils with special needs - in England, Kenya and Germany. She is co-author of an English-language book for use in Kenyan schools and after completing her MSc, worked as an educational psychologist. After travelling and working in Latin America, she now works for the Nicaragua Solidarity Campaign.

GUY MERCHANT

Guy Merchant has worked as a teacher in multilingual schools in the East Midlands. He has conducted research in multicultural education and has contributed to a wide variety of in-service programmes for teachers. He was co-ordinator of the EC pilot project Linguistic Diversity in the Primary School (LDIP) based at the University of Nottingham School of Education, and is now (1989) Senior Lecturer in Language in Education at the University of Sheffield.

PETER TRAVES

Peter Traves is the English Adviser for the London Borough of Waltham Forest. He worked for many years as a teacher in the ILEA and was for a time an Advisory Teacher with ILEA's English team. He has written articles and taken part in radio and television programmes on multicultural education. He has also written on the teaching of literature and has contributed an article to the recently published *Learning Me Your Language* (Mary Glasgow Publications, 1988) which is a response to the current debate about English.

LORNITA YUEN-FAN WONG

Lornita Yuen-Fan Wong taught English language at the secondary level in Hong Kong for three years after her graduation from the Chinese University of Hong Kong. From 1983 she taught the Chinese language for four years at various schools in London after school hours. She has also served as a voluntary community worker and as member of the Executive Committee of the Haringey Chinese Community Centre London. Her research interest is in the linguistic and cultural aspects of ethnic minority people in a plural society. Her article is part of her PHD thesis on the education of Chinese children in Britain and the United States.

Glossary

Part of this glossary has been based on <u>Brief</u>, the list of acronyms and abbreviations in education issued by the NFER, and we gratefully acknowledge this source.

B Ed (Bachelor of Education) - A first degree awarded by a university or by the Council for National Academic Awards after an approved course.

Bilingualism - The ability to use more than one language to a reasonable degree of competence in a variety of situations, but not necessarily with equal facility in both languages. In Britain, bilingual skills are normally understood as skills in English and at least one other language.

Bullock Report - The report (*A language for life*, 1975) of the Committee of Inquiry into Reading and the use of English, which was established by the Secretary of State for Education and Science to consider, in relation to schools, all aspects of teaching the use of English, and to make recommendations on improving practice and monitoring attainment.

CPVE (Certificate of Pre-Vocational Education) - A national qualification for 16-17 years age range. One-year courses available in school and college to prepare students for a future job, or more vocational training.

Community language - The language of distinct areas or cultural areas within a country, but having its origins outside the country in which the community using it lives. A community language may be the mother tongue (*q.v.*) or first language, i.e. the language first used in the home. Children who speak these languages will use them regularly both within and outside the home.

Cox Report - The report (*English for ages 5 to 11*, 1988) of a Working Group established in April 1988 to advise on attainment targets, programmes of study and associated assessment arrangements for English (language and literature) in the National Curriculum (*q.v.*) for the period of compulsory schooling.

ESG (Education Support Grant) - The Grant is paid by Central Government to LEAs (*q.v.*) to encourage them to divert a limited amount of expenditure into specific activities named by the Government, which are intended to promote improvements in the education service and to assist local education authorities to respond to changing demands.

ESL (English as a second language) - English when used by a speaker whose mother tongue is not English, in a country where English is the dominant language for day-to-day business in school and outside the home.

Examination modes - Mode 1 - In which the Examination Board issues the syllabus, sets the papers and marks the scripts.

Mode 2 - Permits a school to submit a syllabus for approval by the Examination Board which, after approval, sets and marks the examination papers.

Mode 3 - The school submits a syllabus for approval by the Examination Board, and on approval sets and marks its own examination; the Board reviews the scripts and makes final decisions.

GCSE (General Certificate of Secondary Education) - From 1988, replaces GCE 'O' level (General Certificate of Education ordinary level, taken at age 16) and CSE (Certificate of Secondary Education) as the main examination system in English secondary schools.

Graded Objectives in Modern Languages (GOML) - A system of short-term objectives for the teaching and assessment of modern languages and increasingly adopted by other areas of the curriculum. Akin to stage-related examinations for musical or gymnastic performance.

GRIST (Grant-Related In-Service Training) - Specific funding from the Department of Education and Science to local education authorities for in-service training of teachers. Now called Local Education Authorities Training Grants Scheme (LEATGS).

HMI (Her Majesty's Inspectorate (of Schools)) - Reports to the Secretary of State for Education and Science on the state of the education system by carrying out inspections. All educational establishments are covered, including independent schools.

Heritage language - A language supported because of the importance of its linguistic and cultural heritage. The origins may be from any part of the world, and the language may not be in current use by the learner with cultural connections.

ILEA (Inner London Education Authority) - At present (1988), a local education authority (*see* LEA) of ten divisions comprising the inner boroughs of London. From 1990, the ILEA will split up into its constituent boroughs, which will then be responsible for administering their own educational provision.

INSET (In-Service Education and Training of Teachers) - Training or activity undertaken by a teacher as part of professional development. It can be school based or undertaken as part of a recognised course.

Kingman Report - Report (1988) of the Committee of Inquiry into the Teaching of English Language established to recommend a model of the English language which would serve as a basis for training teachers to understand how the language works and to guide them in transmitting this knowledge to pupils. On this basis, the Committee also recommends what pupils need to know about the English language at ages 7, 11 and 16.

LEA (Local Education Authority) - Body charged with overseeing the state-maintained educational system in its own area of the country.

Licensed Teacher Grade - The non-standard route to QTS (*q.v.*); an intermediate category between unqualified and qualified teacher. An employer (usually the LEA or a school governing body) may recommend that a person be granted a licence to teach at a specified school or for a specified employer, with the understanding that that person fulfils certain minimum requirements and is a candidate for full QTS.

Mother tongue - The individual child's first language of contact, usually in the home, before entering school, and the one to which the speakers may feel the closest emotional attachment, even when it is not the language of which the speaker has the best and most natural command. May also be the community language (*q.v.*).

National Curriculum - A framework of core subjects, foundation subjects and additional subjects required by the central Government for ages 5 -16, with attainment targets prescribed by the Government and assessed at ages 7, 11 and 14. A modern foreign language is included in the list of foundation subjects, although how far the term applies to the community languages in Britain, for example, is not clear. The framework was formally established in the Education Reform Act 1988.

NPRA (Northern Partnership for Records of Achievement) - A two- year pilot study by the Northern Examining Association and the Northern LEAs, which aims to develop and make available for schools and colleges a range of methods for observing, assessing and recording students' achievement in the academic, practical and personal fields.

PGCE (Post-Graduate Certificate in Education) - A qualification obtained at a college or university department of education, which is necessary to enable a graduate to enter the teaching profession.

QTS (Qualified Teacher Status) - A certification of fitness to teach issued by the Department of Education and Science, which teachers must obtain before they may be employed at a school maintained by an LEA (*q.v.*) in England and Wales.

Section 11 - A section of the Local Government Act of 1966 which provides for Central Government to pay 75% of the cost of staff employed by a local authority to meet the special needs of Commonwealth immigrants. It is often used to help fund the Teaching of English as a second language, and before 1986 was sometimes approved for funding the teaching of community languages. Since 1986, community language schemes have not been approved, although those approved before 1986 have been allowed to continue.

Swann Report - The Report (*Education for all*, 1985) of the Committee of Inquiry into the Education of Children from Ethnic Minority Groups which considered, in relation to schools, the

children's educational needs and attainments and made recommendations on the most effective use of resources.

Other CILT publications of interest to teachers of ESL and community languages

Community languages: sources and resources
Compiled and edited by June Geach
The book provides information on organisations and associations, periodicals, an annotated list of published works, a section on teachers' centres in the ESL/CL/multicultural field and an annotated section on specialist publishers. The introduction reviews the current issues against which the contents have been selected.

English as a second language: sources and resources
Compiled and edited by June Geach
A guide for teachers of English to children and adults. Contents include: details of relevant organisations and associations; periodicals; selected annotated list of relevant published works; and a section on the activities and services of teachers' centres in the ESL/CL/multicultural field.

Multilingual Britain: the educational challenge
By Michael Marland
This book is a contribution to the discussion on the education needs of a multilingual society. It attempts to offer a detailed, flexible and readily understandable programme for action. Part 1, *Towards a curriculum policy for a multilingual world*, is the revised text of a paper given to the JCLA in 1986; Part II, *The education of bilingual learners*, is an edited version of the report of a working party on bilingual education.

Teaching Britain's community languages: materials and methods
By Marion Molteno
This book will help the practising teacher to select and provide suitable materials for the widely varying needs of the learners. The examples are taken from Urdu, but the problems discussed are common to the teaching of most community languages in Britain.

Britain's South Asian languages
By Michael Mobbs
An introduction to the principal languages spoken by people of South Asian origin living in Britain.

Write for further details of these and other publications to CILT, Regent's College, Inner Circle , Regent's Park, London NW1 4NS.